Encouraged b
he visited the English lord
taken prisoner a
He gave the whole
Chronicles of France, England, Scotland, Spain,
Brittany and Flanders.
It took the story up to·the end of the
14th century, the major part dealing with
the Hundred Years' War.
A brilliant chronicler and historian,
Froissart recorded the most minute details
bearing on these historic events.

Þ ſnque boit
nonnables et
nobles auen
turrs faittes
varmes leſquelles ſont adue
nuꝛ par les guerres de frace
et dangleterre ſoyent noble
ment regiſtrees 2 miſes en
memoire ſans ſin parquoy
les preuw ayent exemple
deuld enculurraitier en fat
ſant bien. Ie ueuil traitter

et recorder hiſtoire 2 matiere
de grant loenge. laquelle ſa
deuiſe en quatre parties.
Mais ains que ie ſa commie
ce ie requiers au ſauueour de
tout le monde qui de neant
aa toutes choſes qͥ il ueuil
le creer 2 mettre en moy ſes
2 entendement ſy ſebrueuſy
que ce liure qͥ iay commencie
ie puiſſe continuer et preſer
ter en belle maniere qͥ tous

The author at his desk, with a battle scene in the background.

The army of Edward III crossing the Tyne to fight the Scots.

The sea battle of Guernsey in 1342 with armed ships locked in close combat.

bataille La furt enclos et
combatus aſprement et ne
peurent porter le fais des
francois Si y furet prins
z douloureuſemet naure
meſſ. thomas dagorne et ſe
ſauua le mielx quil peut
les meſſ. iehan de hurtenel
le auecques vne partie
de ſes hommes · Mais la
greigneur partie deulx y
demourerent mors naure
z prins. Et retourna
d'cellui meſſire iehan de
hurteuelle auec ceulx qui

eſchupper peurent ſur la
riuiere · Si racompta A
meſſ. tanguy du chaſteau
tout au long ſo auanture
Si eurent conſeil quilz
ſen retourneroiet deuers
hambont ·

Cy parle de bataille de la
roche dirien. Et com
ment meſſire charles de
blois fut pris des anglois.

Battle of the Derrien Rock, with the capture of
Charles de Blois in 1347.

Peasants are cut to pieces and thrown into the Marne
at Meaux by Gaston de Foix.

The coronation of Charles V and Jeanne de Bourbon
at Rheims in 1364.

CONTENTS

WRITING
THE STORY OF ALPHABETS AND SCRIPTS

Georges Jean

THAMES AND HUDSON

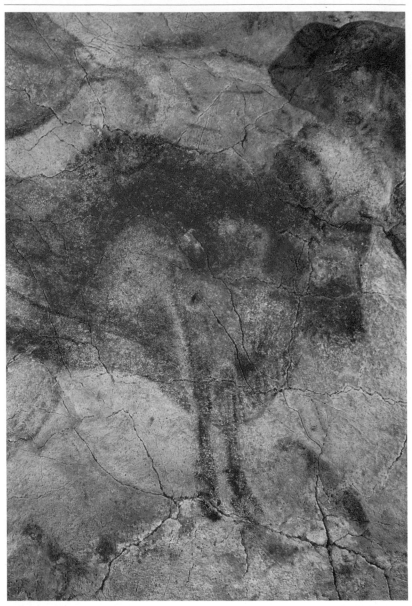

Almost twenty-two thousand years ago, in the caves at Lascaux, human beings produced the first pictures. It was to be another seventeen millennia before mankind's most extraordinary achievement, the art of writing, made its appearance. One might imagine that people thought up the first written signs in order to preserve their traditional stories. In reality, the reasons behind the development of writing are much more mundane.

CHAPTER 1
HUMBLE BEGINNINGS

"Although man has been living and dying for a million years, he has only been writing for six thousand years."
René Etiemble

Over tens of thousands of years there were many means of conveying simple messages using drawings, signs or pictures. Writing, however, in the true sense of the word, cannot be said to exist until there is an agreed repertoire of formal signs or symbols that can be used to reproduce clearly the thoughts and feelings the writer wishes to express.

Such a system does not appear overnight, and the history of writing is a long, slow-moving and complicated process. It is also a fascinating story, inextricably bound up with the history of man himself, a story from which many important episodes are still lacking.

As far as we know, the process began in ancient Mesopotamia, the land between the Tigris and Euphrates rivers. This area of the Middle East, which stretches from the Persian Gulf northwards to Baghdad (capital of modern Iraq), was, around the 3rd millennium BC, divided into Sumer in the south, and Akkad in the north.

Reliable records of accounts cannot be kept orally – and so writing is born of practical necessity

Although the Sumerians and Akkadians lived harmoniously within the same geographical area, they spoke two languages as drastically different from one another as English and Chinese. These two highly civilized societies lived in small communities clustered around larger cities, such as Babylon, controlled by their rulers and protected by their deities. Beyond the officials of the royal court, the priests and the merchants, the population of Mesopotamia consisted largely of shepherds and farmers. This explains the

The term *calculi* refers to pebbles with geometric designs, which were used for counting. It comes from the Latin *calculus*, meaning 'stone'. The examples below, found at Susa, date from the Neolithic period.

Among the oldest examples of writing found is this tablet from Uruk dating to the end of the 4th millennium BC. This particular tablet bears a lexical text arranged in columns, listing objects made of wood.

first inscriptions found on clay tablets from Sumer, from the great temple complex at the site of Uruk. These Uruk tablets, which constitute a form of written temple records, list sacks of grain and heads of cattle.

The first written signs were therefore used for agricultural accounts. Other later tablets contain information about the social structure of the Sumerians – we learn, for example, that the religious community of the temple at Lagash employed 18 bakers, 31 brewers, 7 slaves and a blacksmith. Other documents show that the Sumerians not only used a silver standard in their transactions, but also developed a system for letting money at interest. Finally, thanks to tablets found in the Sumerian schools with the teacher's text on one side and the pupil's copy on the other, it has been possible to trace how people learned to write cuneiform.

The first inscriptions in this 'writing', which, according to the experts, is rather a form of *aide-mémoire*, consist of simplified drawings used to create stylized representations of objects. For example, the head of a cow was used to indicate 'cow' (fig. 1); a pubic triangle with a trace for the vulva represented 'woman' (fig. 2), and so on. These are pictograms, each sign referring to a particular object or entity.

By combining several pictograms, it became possible to express an idea, and so to form what is sometimes referred to as an ideogram. For example, the sign for

This square tablet with rounded corners (opposite), dating to about 2360 BC, has the characteristic appearance of a so-called Early Dynastic III tablet. It is an economic document concerning the loan of donkeys to various people, including a farmer, a smith and a currier. The sign for 'donkey', with its ears pointing backwards and its long head and neck, is easily recognizable. The sign for 'god' can be seen clearly twice in the lower righthand corner.

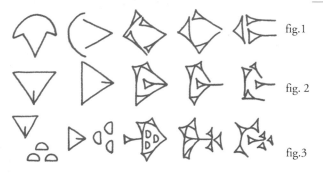

fig.1

fig. 2

fig.3

'mountains' added to that of a pubic triangle represented the idea of a foreign woman, i.e. one who had come from the other side of the mountains – meaning 'female slave' (fig. 3). Scholars have identified some fifteen hundred different early pictograms.

As time passes, the pictograms cease to represent exclusively the objects that they illustrate, and begin to take broader meanings from the context

One particularly interesting development occurred in about 2900 BC; the curves in the primitive pictographic signs disappeared. The reason for this was again a very

basic one. In the riverine and marshy areas of
Mesopotamia there was an abundance of clay and reeds.
It is technically difficult to draw curves on wet clay,
so the script rapidly evolved into signs formed purely
of straight lines.

The scribes who created the inscriptions used clay
tablets, on which they drew the objects or figures that
they wished to depict using a stylus made of a reed with

Styluses, made out of
perishable materials
such as reeds or wood,
have usually not
survived, but
investigation of the
tablets themselves shows
that all wedges can be
written with a tool of
triangular section.

one shaped end. The Sumerians took to cutting these
styluses – forerunners of our quill pens and fountain
pens – with a tip of triangular section. The impressions
printed on the soft clay were therefore in the form of
wedges, and these were used to build up signs based on
the earliest drawings. From this characteristic appearance
comes the name of the writing, cuneiform, from the
Latin *cuneus*, meaning 'wedge'.

Over the centuries there were numerous changes in
the script, to the point where the pictographic origins
became totally obscured. One should not be misled into
thinking that the form of the signs was left to the

Round numerals,
however, must have
been written with the
other, unshaped end
of the reed.

16

discretion of individual scribes. Groups of 'sign-lists' have been found, which were obviously used by the scribes as an early dictionary and aid to learning. Each sign could have several meanings, depending on the

context; the sign that represents a human foot could be understood as 'to walk', 'to stand up', 'to move', etc., each with a different sound and reading. As each sign came to stand for more than its original simple meaning, so the number of signs in the repertoire diminished. Soon there

were no more than about six hundred signs in common use, although this still represented an enormous effort of memory for those who knew how to write.

The rebus: a childish game that was to become the keystone of true writing

A still more extraordinary development was yet to come. The signs impressed by the scribes onto tablets of moist clay, which were then left to dry in the sun, and on rare occasions baked in furnaces, represented things or entities. A significant step in the progress of writing occurred when the signs came to represent the sounds of the spoken language.

The representation of sounds lies at the root of all true writing. The remarkable achievement of the Sumerians, and elsewhere the Egyptians, was to make use of a system as simple as a child's game: the rebus. They came on the idea of using a pictogram, not to represent the object itself, but rather the sounds that made up its name – as if, for instance, one wrote 'carpet' using drawings of a 'car' and a 'pet'. The Sumerian pictogram for an arrow, 'ti', was used to write 'life', for which the word was also 'ti'. This is only one of the simplest examples; phonetic usage as it developed

The pictographs for trees, sacks of grain and farming implements can readily be made out on this tablet from southern Mesopotamia. The sign for 'hand' in the upper right corner perhaps indicates a mark of ownership. The tablet dates to the end of the 4th millennium BC.

Cuneiform inscriptions are also found on monuments and statues, such as this votive dog from Sumer dating to about 1900 BC. It was dedicated to Ninisinna, the goddess who 'hearkens to prayer'.

over time became extremely elaborate. Occasionally Sumerian scribes also used what we call determinative signs to indicate whether a given sign should be read phonetically or as a pictogram.

Law codes, scientific treatises and literary works: writing could now cope with them all

The Akkadians, Semitic ancestors of the Arabs and the Hebrews, eventually came to be the dominant power in Mesopotamia. Their influence was such that, shortly after 2000 BC, Akkadian became

Pictograms could represent ideas as well as objects.

A bird and an egg side by side meant 'fertility'.

Several strokes descending from heaven meant 'night'.

Crossed lines meant 'enmity'.

Parallel lines meant 'friendship'.

the principal spoken language in Mesopotamia. Once cuneiform writing was fully evolved, it was sufficiently flexible to be able to record other languages than merely Akkadian and Sumerian. As Sumerian fell out of use as a spoken language, it was preserved in religious contexts, much as Latin was within the Catholic church. In time this writing system became that of the kingdom of Babylon, which rose to power in the 18th century BC, and of the mighty kingdom of Assyria.

From its humble beginnings as an accounting system, writing gradually became, among the people of Mesopotamia, first, a form of memorandum, then a system for recording spoken language, and, above all, an alternative medium for communication, thought and expression. In this fashion the ancient Sumerians, the Akkadians, the Babylonians and the Assyrians developed correspondence, a postal service, and even clay envelopes.

Among many other significant achievements, the invention of cuneiform allowed the preservation of hymns, divination texts, and what we have to describe as literature. The ancient Sumerians, for example, composed the *Epic of Gilgamesh*, which tells of a solar giant, 'two-thirds god and one-third man'. It first circulated in oral form, and many later written fragments have been recovered, largely from the library of the Assyrian king

Development of the sign for king (man + crown) between 2500 and 600 BC.

Early Dynastic III period, *c.* 2500 BC.

Akkadian period, *c.* 2250 BC.

Ur III period, *c.* 2150 BC.

Old Babylonian period, *c.* 1760 BC.

Neo-Assyrian period, *c.* 720 BC.

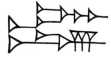

Monumental Assyrian form, *c.* 7th century BC.

This stela records a donation made by the Babylonian king Marduk-Zakir-Shumi (9th century BC), who is shown in the centre holding a staff. In front of him stands the recipient, a scribe at the great temple of Eanna, in Uruk, who was entrusted with the task of 'pacifying the heart of the gods'. Behind the king, among various divine symbols, appears the stylus of Nabu, god of scribes. This is called the *qantuppi*, literally 'tablet reed'.

Beneath the overflowing vase of waters carried by Gudea, ruler of Lagash (opposite, far left), is an inscription dedicated to Geshtinanna, the goddess 'of life-giving water'. Southern Mesopotamia, 2150 BC.

Assurbanipal (669–627 BC) at Nineveh. This epic, which anticipates the great Greek myths, in particular the Labours of Hercules, also contains an extraordinary retelling of the Flood story, foreshadowing the account in the Bible.

This stela, a reconstruction of which is shown on the right, is one of the rare representations of Assyrian scribes. Two of them are listing booty from the sack of Musasir in Urartu, during the eighth campaign of King Sargon II (722–705) in 714 BC, to an official seated in front of them. The Assyrian scribe, who is writing in cuneiform on a clay tablet, stands in front of an Aramean scribe, who is unrolling his parchment.

Despite its evolution towards increased simplicity, writing is still restricted to a very small number of people

The reading and writing of cuneiform was not a straightforward matter for the ancient Mesopotamians. It was an art confined to those who knew how to inscribe the signs, and who understood the various meanings they might have, depending on the context. Both in Babylon and in Assur, in Assyria, scribes to a certain extent constituted a caste apart, sometimes, perhaps, becoming more powerful than the illiterate courtiers or even the sovereign himself. The elite scribal

The inscription on the upper part of the relief, which is not reproduced in this drawing, is very damaged and hard to read, but its meaning can be recovered with the help of parallel texts. It is an extract from the annals of Sargon II: '[and these nations] bore my yoke... Merodach-Baladan of the Bit-Yakin tribe, king of Chaldea ... relying on the river Amer and the great floods [to defend them] reneged on his promise and withheld tribute...'.

schools were rigorously disciplined, as is witnessed by numerous documents and the many exercise tablets of Mesopotamian pupils which have survived. Knowing how to write was already a source of considerable power. This knowledge was to remain a privilege.

The writing system of Mesopotamia is used to transcribe vastly different languages from the ones for which it was originally created

A far-reaching implication of this first writing system was that it could be used to write languages other than Sumerian and Akkadian. For example, Elamite, the language of Elam, whose capital was Susa (in modern

Iran), was written with cuneiform characters.
Even more surprising is the fact that the Hittites
of Anatolia (present-day Turkey), a rich and
powerful civilization during the period
1400–1200 BC, adopted a simplified cuneiform
with great success, even though
their language was an Indo-
European one, and despite the
fact that they also developed their
own unique pictographic writing
system. Another example is 'Old
Persian', which was used in the
Persian empire (approximately
corresponding to modern-day
Iran) – at its height around 500
BC – and which was written in
a cuneiform alphabet derived from
the Mesopotamian sign forms.

Between the 3rd and 1st
millennia BC cuneiform writing,
invented between the Tigris and
the Euphrates, travelled as far
south as Palestine, and as far north
as Armenia, where it recorded
respectively Canaanite and
Urartian. Had the cuneiform
writing system not been adopted
by the surrounding countries of
the Middle East, it is unlikely that
scholars would ever have been able
to penetrate their history.

When scribes wrote
on metal they
used a special stylus.
This silver plaque (left)
of Darius I, king of
Persia (522–486 BC),
exemplifies the later use
of cuneiform and
demonstrates its
adaptability, since here
it is used to write
Babylonian (middle
section), Elamite
(righthand section)
and Old Persian
(lefthand section).
Hittite hieroglyphs
(below), on the other
hand, which were clearly
pictographic, were
adopted in Anatolia
around the 14th
century BC.

While cuneiform signs were spreading throughout Mesopotamia, other writing systems were appearing and being developed in nearby Egypt and distant China. From one end of the world to the other, man, seeing writing as a divine gift, set himself to record his past on stone, clay and papyrus.

CHAPTER 2

INVENTION OF THE GODS

Divine figures: Re Horakhty, to whom the harpist dedicates his music, and Thoth, the god of writing and patron of Egyptian scribes, who guides Nebmertuf in his reading.

The history of Egypt would undoubtedly have remained largely unknown had Jean-François Champollion and the Egyptologists been unable to penetrate the secrets of the hieroglyphic writing that covers countless monuments in the Nile delta.

This group of hieroglyphs appears in a cartouche, i.e. a frame that indicates a sacred name, in this case that of Rameses IX, king of Upper and Lower Egypt in the 12th century BC.

A fragment from the *Book of the Dead*, the strip of hieroglyphs opposite reads from top to bottom. Two scarab signs, meaning 'to come into existence', can be seen. Between them appears the sign for mouth, meaning 'to speak'. Since this passage is fragmentary it is difficult to give a translation.

This style of writing, in contrast to cuneiform writing, which appears rather austere, geometric and abstract, is poetic, fascinating – indeed, almost alive – because it is created from beautifully stylized drawings: human heads, birds, a variety of animals, plants and flowers.

The Sumerians and the ancient Egyptians inhabited the same part of the world, and their civilizations had much in common. To this day scholars debate the possible connections between Mesopotamian pictograms and Egyptian hieroglyphs. However, this discussion remains largely hypothetical, and research is far from complete.

According to the ancient Egyptians, it was the god Thoth who created writing and then bestowed it as a gift on mankind

The word 'hieroglyph', which refers to the characters used in the writing of the ancient Egyptians, in fact means 'writing of the gods' (from the Greek *hieros*, meaning 'holy', and *gluphein*, 'to engrave'). The earliest known hieroglyphic inscriptions date back to the 3rd millennium BC, but the script must have originated well before that. It underwent no major changes until AD 390, when Egypt was under the power of the Romans, although over the centuries the number of signs increased from approximately seven hundred to around five thousand.

In contrast to the neighbouring Sumerians, the Egyptians create a writing system that is more immediately capable of expressing everything they want to record

Whereas the early inscriptions of Mesopotamia only gradually developed from a form of *aide-mémoire* into a flexible writing system, the hieroglyphic system was from the beginning a true form of writing: first, because it could almost completely record the spoken language (a language that can be partially recovered, insofar as it has survived in the form of Coptic); and second, due to its ability to deal with abstract, as well as concrete entities and to transcribe equally well texts concerning agriculture, medicine, law and education, religious prayers, traditional stories and, indeed, literature in all its forms.

The originality and complexity of this writing system are largely due to the fact that in the main it is made up of three kinds of sign: pictograms – stylized drawings representing objects or beings, with combinations of

As well as providing a meaningful text, these hieroglyphs from the walls of the temple of Karnak at Thebes enhance the beauty of the sculpted figures.

Phonetic signs can be classed into three categories: alphabetic, biliteral and triliteral. The sign shown below is a biliteral example to be read 'hn'.

the same signs to express ideas; phonograms – the same or different forms used to represent sounds (the Egyptians used a rebus system similar to that of the early Sumerians); and finally determinatives – signs used to indicate which category of objects or beings is in question.

For those deciphering the 'writing of the gods', enjoyment of its beauty increases the pleasure of understanding it

This graphic system, a specific style of writing, was truly the 'writing of the gods'. Generally, divine names and those of the pharaohs (who were seen as gods) appear in the texts in the form of cartouches, so that the sacred character of these words is immediately recognizable.

Most commonly, lines of hieroglyphs were written to be read from right to left. And this direction was

signalled by the direction of the human and birds' heads; the person reading was intended to move his eyes the same way.

In practice, it was not always that simple. For example, if an inscription on the wall of a monument or temple were located near the statue of an important god (e.g. Osiris or Anubis), or of a pharaoh, the faces in the inscription would be turned towards the statue, thus seemingly changing the direction of reading and making the text more difficult to understand. Hieroglyphs could also be written from bottom to top or in alternating directions: right to left on one line and then left to right on the following line. This latter style of writing is called *boustrophedon*, meaning, literally, as an ox travels back and forth when ploughing the fields.

Hieroglyphs are somehow universally fascinating. The countless deities of ancient Egypt are glorified in hieroglyphs covering temple walls and tombs. It is almost as if the hieroglyphs themselves were sacred. These signs, whether engraved in stone or painted, have a beauty surpassing the merely human, and seem, irrespective of what is actually written, to be pure 'visual poems'. In the eyes of the ancient Egyptians, they could only be of divine inspiration. And for us, too, contemplating these wonders, they produce an effect akin to great poetry or (for a believer) prayer.

This group of hieroglyphs is to be read, unusually, from left to right. The first sign on the left reads 'hb'. The second is a determinative; the leg indicates that the word in question concerns the foot. The third is a figurative pictogram showing a dancing man. The whole means 'to dance'.

Although essentially divine in character, hieroglyphs are not devoted exclusively to religious uses

The innumerable monuments and documents found in Egypt bear witness, as does cuneiform writing, to many aspects of a highly developed civilization. Writing made it possible for the ancient Egyptians to record their own history, to draw up lists of their kings and to recount

The basic unit of measurement, this royal rule, is a royal cubit (52 cm), which is divided into twenty-eight 'fingers' of 1.86 cm. These are themselves grouped into four 'palms' of 7.44 cm.

important events – for example, royal marriages or wars. In Egypt, as everywhere else, history was born with writing, in that for the first time events could be established in chronological order. The writing system they had developed, however, served equally well for

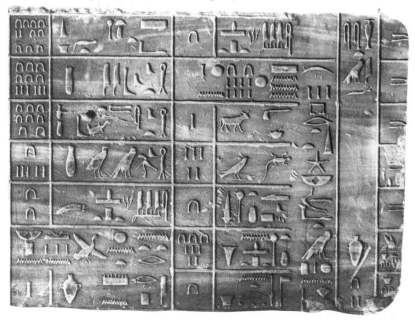

recording accounts (as in the case of the early Sumerians), for drawing up legal codes and marriage contracts, or drafting bills for the sale of goods.

It served also as a medium for literature. Ancient Egyptian literature possesses an extraordinary richness, combining very diverse elements, including moral maxims, hymns to gods and kings, historical sagas and adventure stories, love songs, epic poetry and fables. Among the best known of these monuments of ancient

The Elephantine calendar (opposite, below) was engraved during the reign of Tuthmosis I (c. 1450 BC). It lists offerings that were to be presented annually to the gods on the day when the Sothic star (our Sirius) rose on the horizon. Its appearance is marked by a date: the twenty-eighth day of the third month of summer. The star is shown in the middle of the third column from the right.

On the Goldmine papyrus, dating to the 20th dynasty (c. 1100 BC), four chains of mountain peaks are shown. At the top are the granite 'gold-mountains', with their gold-producing mines. Below them stand the small houses of the workmen; on the right, in white, is the temple of the god Amun, and below, the main road is marked out with rocks and stones.

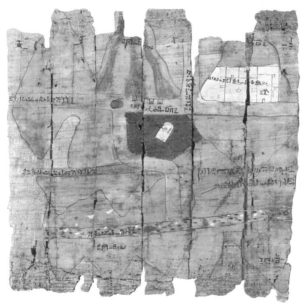

Egyptian literature is the *Book of the Dead*, written in hieroglyphs under the 19th dynasty, during the 13th century BC.

Neither should we overlook the geographical and scientific texts, those dealing with the arts of divination, magic, medicine, pharmacopoeia, cookery, astronomy and the measurement of time. The calendar, formerly based on the moon, became a solar calendar in the 3rd millennium, comprising 365¼ days a year, and this change was recorded in detail by the Egyptians.

Weighing the soul

Under the 19th dynasty the dead were entombed with a copy of the *Book of the Dead* as a provision on their journey to Eternity. During the burial ceremony a reading was made from this book by a priest. Taking the form of a roll of papyrus, leather or linen, decorated with beautifully coloured vignettes, each book was entitled the 'Book of the Coming Forth to Daylight'. The texts that it contained depicted in great detail the stages of rebirth, one of which was the weighing of the soul. The dead man's heart was put in one pan of a balance, and on the other was placed the Feather of Maat (symbolizing Justice and Truth); the two had to balance. In this illustration the centre figure is the jackal-headed god Thoth, who was in charge of the weighing process. 'The Great Devourer', the hybrid creature seated to the right, is ready to tear the man to pieces if the judgment is unfavourable. The background is covered with hieroglyphs describing the scene.

Khnum and the gods of the Underworld

This section introduces us to a fantasy world: the dead person (on the left) presents himself before the ram-headed god of the Underworld, Khnum. A strange two-headed creature and a serpent are also present. Around this scene are written charms that will enable the dead person to repel the serpent and to avoid being eaten by worms. Texts of the *Book of the Dead* reflect how the word and writing had a magical connotation, since their presence by the side of the dead person guaranteed his resurrection.

Dead woman worshipping a crocodile

Once released, the dead person could enjoy the pleasures of the 'Field of Reeds', the Egyptian paradise. The pictures and texts relating to this stage protect the dead on the journey to Eternity; they include charms to help them to avoid dying a second time, and to allay the primitive fear of having to walk upside down. There are also ritual images evoking scenes similar to those of the living world; here a dead woman prostrates herself before the crocodile Sobek, god of fertility, summoning the Nile floods through his mediation.

This painted limestone model with inlaid eyes made of alabaster, rock crystal and ebony shows a seated scribe at work under the 4th dynasty (2620–2520 BC). The extraordinary concentration of his pose and the intensity of his expression, the very stillness of this figure poised to begin writing, make this a timeless image of man the writer.

The illustration above shows a text in cursive hieratic with several implements of the scribal art: on the left, a box containing the sharpened reeds, and below, the board on which the scribe smoothed out his papyrus and on which he leaned to write. The two wells were filled with black and red ink (the red was for writing the names of gods). On the right is a papyrus knife.

In Egypt, as in Mesopotamia, knowing how to read and write is both a mark of privilege and a source of power

The Egyptian scribes were of course masters of the art of writing and therefore masters of teaching – for teaching meant almost exclusively the teaching of writing. Considering the number of signs that had to be memorized and the great complexity of the hieroglyphic system, it must have been a hard task. Boys entered school when they were about ten years old. Most spent only a few years there, but the most gifted students continued their studies until they were adults.

The teaching methods of the Egyptian masters combined exercises from memory with written work and reading; pupils spent much of their time chanting in unison. The art of writing was taught through dictation and the copying of exercises, initially using the cursive script and later, hieroglyphs. Corporal

These trainee scribes are shown carrying out a writing exercise at their master's dictation. Each holds the stylus in his right hand and the papyrus roll in his left.

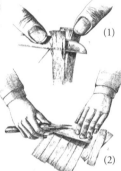

(1)

(2)

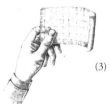

(3)

punishment was considered an effective means of education, if one is to believe the Egyptian saying: 'A boy's ears are on his back; he listens when he is beaten.' For real dunces punishment could be as severe as actual imprisonment.

So the scribes formed a powerful section of society. Their mastery of the art of writing sometimes made them as powerful as the pharaoh for whom they worked, particularly since the kings, content with their status as deities, tended not to bother to learn reading, writing and arithmetic.

Unlike their Mesopotamian counterparts, the Egyptian scribes used diverse media for their writing. Certainly, they engraved hieroglyphs on stone, but they also used another, much more supple, fine and tractable material – papyrus.

Five thousand years ago scribes were already using paper, pen and ink

Papyrus is a plant that grows in great abundance in the marshes of the Nile delta. It was used to make many objects in daily use, such as ropes, matting, sandals and sails. Its fibrous stems enabled the Egyptians to create a material that was to revolutionize the art of writing by creating 'sheets' of paper.

The stems of papyrus were cut into thin strips (1) and then overlapped (2). Sections were then superimposed at right-angles to each other to form sheets (3), and the papyrus was finally smoothed and thinned.

They did this by cutting the stems into thin strips, which were then laid together with their edges overlapping. By putting two layers of these strips together, one on top of the other and at right-angles to it, a supple, flat surface could be achieved, which was then dried under pressure before being polished. Using starch paste, some twenty sheets could be stuck together lengthwise to obtain a roll of papyrus several metres long.

In order to write, the scribe unwound the roll of papyrus with his left hand and wrote the inscriptions on it, re-rolling it with his right hand as he went along. Because of the length of the rolls (the longest found measures 40 m), he usually worked in a cross-legged seated position, with the papyrus wedged on his knees and resting on his loincloth. For writing he used a reed stick, about 20 cm long, with one end either crushed or cut, depending on the desired use. The thick black ink was made of a mixture of water and soot, with the addition of a fixative such as gum arabic. Titles, headings and the beginnings of chapters were written in red ink made of a base of cinnabar (mercuric sulphide) or minium (lead oxide).

The Egyptian state had a monopoly over the making of papyrus. From the 3rd millennium BC papyrus was

In this tomb fresco workers are shown filling sacks of grain, which are being counted by a seated official. The scribes on the right are making notes as they proceed. One of the functions of the Egyptian scribe was to record and distribute the harvests.

exported throughout the Mediterranean region and provided a significant source of revenue.

There was, however, much discontent among the scribes and students in Egypt itself, as the monopoly on the production of papyrus resulted in very high prices. Palimpsests (papyri where the original text has been erased so that the papyrus could be reused), probably bear testimony to the high cost of new papyri.

Limestone and pottery were less costly and served perfectly well as the medium for less important texts. Parchment, already familiar to the Egyptians, was even more expensive than papyrus, and its use was reserved strictly for the most valuable documents.

In response to daily needs, two different and more rapid writing forms develop from the hieroglyphic system

Drawing hieroglyphs on papyrus required very considerable skill and patience. Writing with such highly detailed signs was ill-adapted to daily life and the speed required for certain tasks. So at about the same time as the hieroglyphic system, the scribes also developed a more flowing cursive script. It, too, was called hieratic (from the Greek *hieros*, 'sacred') or sacerdotal, because according to the Greek historian Herodotus (*c.* 424–85), from whom the term comes, this script was originally used by priests.

This cursive writing system contained the same elements as the hieroglyphic one (ideograms, phonograms and determinatives), but as they were often used in compounds, the signs gradually began to diverge from the original pictures.

By about 650 BC, while both the hieroglyphic writing system and the 'cursive hieratic' were still current, a third, quicker, lighter and more ligatured system appeared, which was read, like the hieratic, from right to left. This became known as 'demotic' script – the writing of the people – and was to become the prevalent script in use in Egypt. On the famous Rosetta Stone, from which Jean-François Champollion was able to decipher hieroglyphs, the same text is found written

This funerary stela from the tomb of Nefer and Ka-Hay shows the papyrus harvest. Having been pulled out of the soft earth, the stems were tied in bundles and carried away on the men's backs to be dried.

Papyrus permitted the use of the cursive script, which was unsuitable for harder media such as metal or stone. Hieratic, the cursive script, is almost as old as the hieroglyphic script from which it derives. However, in demotic, the most recent form, one can hardly recognize the original underlying hieroglyphs.

in hieroglyphs, demotic and Greek. For a non-specialist it is extremely difficult to recognize the original hieroglyphs to which the individual demotic signs correspond.

Some traces of this ancient demotic script still persist in use today. Just as it was possible to discover numerous clues to the spoken language of the ancient Egyptians through the study of spoken Coptic, so some

demotic signs have been retained in Coptic script. Hence Champollion's insistence that in order to understand hieroglyphs it was essential to be able to read Coptic.

While the Mesopotamian and Egyptian scripts have yielded up their secrets, the writing of ancient Crete remains a mystery. At the time when cuneiform had reached its definitive form, and while the Egyptian civilization was expanding vastly, leading to a proliferation of hieroglyphic inscriptions, around the 2nd millennium BC there developed in Crete, and doubtless also on the Greek mainland, a writing system that has long posed problems for scholars.

During the mid-19th century the excavators of the ruined Cretan city of Knossos discovered a large

The forty-five signs on the Phaistos disc have been dated to the 17th century BC. The signs are images of animals, objects of daily life and houses. It is thought that the writing begins at the edge of the disc. The number of signs used and the grouping of two or three signs into words make it probable that this is some form of syllabic system.

This Chinese seal (right), made of porcelain with enamel decoration, is a forerunner of printing blocks.

In Chinese writing (opposite, far right), the 'keys', of which there are 214, placed by the side of another character, dictate the meaning of the word as a whole. The element 'to be able' (c) preceded by the key 'water' (a), for example, means 'river' (d). However, the same element associated with the key 'word' (b) produces 'to criticize' (e).

collection of fragmentary inscriptions. These signs were engraved on seals of steatite (a soft, easily worked stone) or impressed on clay, as in the case of the famous Phaistos disc, which remains one of the greatest puzzles in the history of writing. In 1906 Italian archaeologists discovered this large clay disc, which was covered on both faces with forty-five signs written in a spiral. So far, no one has been able to decipher them.

On the other side of the world, in about 2000 BC, the Chinese develop the writing system that is still in use there today

The Chinese writing system is unique; invented in about the 2nd millennium BC, codified around 1500 BC and systemized between 200 BC and AD 200, it remains essentially unchanged today.

Hieroglyphs and cuneiform were supplanted by Arabic writing many centuries ago in Egypt and Mesopotamia (modern Iraq). Chinese writing in contrast has effectively remained unaltered. Admittedly, the Chinese originally wrote with a brush and ink, while today they tend to write with a pen or even a biro. Admittedly also, printing machinery and

(a)

(b)

(c)

(d)

(e)

typewriters are equipped with characters without the (thick) downstrokes or the (thin) upstrokes that originally characterized hand-written Chinese characters. But with the exception of certain modifications made in favour of simplicity, the Chinese writing system has remained very faithful to its original form.

Like the Egyptians, the Chinese attribute a legendary origin to writing

According to legend, three emperors were involved in the birth of writing in China. In particular, the emperor Huang-Che, who lived during the 3rd millennium BC, was supposed to have discovered the gift of writing after studying the heavenly bodies and objects in nature, especially bird and animal footprints. It was the worst of all possible discoveries, if one is to believe the poet Wu-Weiye: 'Huang-Che wept throughout the night, with much cause'.

Much more enlightening was a discovery made in the wake of the flooding of the Yellow River in 1898-9, which brought to light fragments of tortoise shells and deer scapulae. On these fragments were found traces of inscriptions, the oldest known examples of Chinese writing.

Viviane Alleton, an expert in Chinese writing, tells us that 'the priests wrote their questions on one side of the tortoise shell and then held the other side towards a fire (lit in the east); the theory was that the answer to the question could be read from the shapes of the cracks caused by the heat. The characters representing the questions were inscribed from top to bottom in columns. These characters are, both in structure and in their basic constituents, still in use today.'

The pictogram, the initial step and key element in all writing systems, can still be found in Chinese characters

In almost all civilizations the story of writing begins with the same first chapter. In the case of the Chinese

In Chinese and Japanese painting the calligraphy of the characters constitutes a separate semantic element: the style of writing, the colour of the ink and the intensity of each stroke can all contribute to the overall meaning. The manuscripts came in the form of rolls, which were carried on the backs of Buddhist pilgrims (right).

日 ☉

山 ◠

木 米

中 ⊕

田 ⊞

畾 門

門

Certain pictograms dating back to the beginning of Chinese writing have lasted down to modern times. Thirty centuries separate the signs on the right from those on the left. From top to bottom: sun, mountain, tree, middle, field, frontier, door.

– as with the Sumerians, the Egyptians, the Hittites and the Cretans – it is clear that the first signs were invariably drawings, i.e. pictograms and combinations of pictograms. As one might, perhaps, expect, certain

pictograms from the writing systems developed in different parts of the world show remarkable similarities, despite the fact that they originated in vastly different cultures.

Chinese writing conforms to a series of subtle rules which make it a truly poetic art form

Although pictograms rapidly became stylized, traces of the early pictographic elements can still be detected in modern Chinese characters. This lends an extraordinarily poetic aspect to the writing, which comes out particularly in certain sign combinations. For example, the character for 'dragon' added to that for 'ear' means 'deaf'.

The true essence of the written Chinese language is that a single sound can represent several things, depending on how it is written. The sound 'shi', for example, can mean 'to know', 'to be', 'power', 'world', 'oath', 'to leave', 'to put', 'affair', 'to love', 'to see', 'to watch over', 'to count on', 'to walk', 'to try', 'to

The teachings of Buddha on the observance of abstinence and poverty are the subject of this Chinese silk embroidery (above left), dating to the 7th century BC, on which the characters form both the text and the decoration.

explain', 'house' etc., according to the other elements with which it is combined. Usually, each character is formed of a key, which gives the basic meaning, and a phonetic element, which provides guidelines to pronunciation.

Certain aspects of Chinese calligraphy make this script more than merely a system for communicating information. For example, each Chinese character must be circumscribed by a perfect square, and every sign should be written by drawing the individual elements in an exact order. Such careful attention to the visual and graphic qualities of the script means that, as in the case of Arabic writing, Chinese characters can constitute a decorative element of great beauty, and they have frequently formed an integral part of Chinese paintings.

It is the Chinese script, far more than the spoken language (which is different in the north and the south of the country), that forms a unifying element in Chinese culture.

The significance of this 18th-century Chinese silk painting lies in the printed signs, which identify its maker. This printing technique using seals was known to the Chinese long before the invention of printing in Europe.

جَتَى إِذَا أَغْنَزَتْنِي مَوَاهِبُهُ وَأَطَالَ ذَيْلِي ذَهَبُهُ لَطَفْتُ فِي الِارْتِجَالِ عَلَى مَا

تُرَى مِنْ حُضُورِ الجَبَانِ فَقُلْتُ لَهُ فَشُكْرُ المِنَجِ لِلْقِيَانِ السَّبِيحِ الكَرِيمِ

وَانْفَذْ مِنْ ضَعَطِهِ الغَرِيمَ   فَقَالَ الحَمْدُ لِلَّهِ عَلَى سَعَادَةِ الجِدِّ وَالخُلُوصِ

مِنَ الخَصْمِ الأَلَدِّ ثُمَّ قَالَ إِلَيْكَ يَا حَبِيبِ أَنْ أَجَذِيَكَ مِنَ العَطَاءِ أَمْ أُحْفِلُكَ بِالمَالِ فَإِنَّ

الرَّقِيطَ آثَرَ فَلَنْ أَمْلَأَ الرِّسَالَةَ اجْتَالَى فَقَالَ وَهُوَ وَجَفَلَ خَضَعَ عَلَيَّ فَإِنْ

نِخْلَةُ مَا لِجَ فِي الآذَانِ أَهْوَنُ مِنْ نِخْلَةِ مَا يَخْرُجُ مِنَ الأَرْدَانِ ثُمَّ كَانَ أَنِفَ

وَاسْتَحْيَى فَجَمَعَ إِلَيَّ بَيْنَ الرِّسَالَةِ وَالجَبَّا فَقَرَنْتُ مِنْهُ سَهْمَيْنِ وَفَصَلْتُ عَنْهُ بِغْنَمَيْنِ

وَأُبْتُ إِلَى وَطَنِي قَرِيرَ العَيْنِ

بِمَا جِئْتُ مِنَ الرِّسَالَةِ وَالعَيْنِ

One thousand years before Christ there occurred a crucial upheaval in the history of writing – the alphabet was invented. It was not an instantaneous event, but the result of a long history. At its roots were the Phoenicians, a people who had gradually spread across the western shores of the Mediterranean, as far as North Africa and southern Spain, into Sicily, Sardinia, Cyprus and even Greece and Italy.

CHAPTER 3

THE ALPHABET REVOLUTION

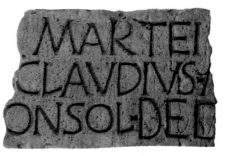

Arabic and Latin scripts lie behind many alphabets. This Arabic text (left) by the 13th-century poet Al-Hariri reads from right to left, while the Roman inscription of the 3rd century (right) reads from left to right.

One feature shared by cuneiform, hieroglyphs and Chinese characters was that all three could be used to transcribe either words or syllables. In order to be able to read or write any of these systems it was therefore necessary to master a large number of signs or characters.

An alphabet functions quite differently. In principle, it should be possible to write anything by using only about thirty signs. Obviously, it is not quite as straightforward as this. The twenty-six letters of our alphabet, for instance, do not allow us to transcribe all the sounds in our language, hence many of the problems encountered by children learning to spell. All the same, twenty-six letters is considerably fewer than the thousand basic signs needed for writing Chinese, the hundreds of hieroglyphs used in Egyptian, or the six hundred cuneiform signs that the student scribe in Mesopotamia would have had to memorize. It was, therefore, according to some thinkers, only with the advent of the alphabet that learning could become available to ordinary people.

In the 14th century BC at Ugarit, near Byblos on the coast of Syria, a remarkable cuneiform script using only twenty-two signs was developed. The signs were all consonants, and the vowels, which were not written down, were supplied by the reader. This in fact constitutes the first alphabetic writing. The tablet below left shows the Ugaritic cuneiform alphabet.

The inscription on this stone (below) discovered in Sardinia, and apparently dating to the 9th century BC, bears witness to the geographical spread of the first non-cuneiform alphabet, which appeared in Phoenicia about 1200 BC.

The first alphabet, that of the Phoenicians, omitted all vowels

The Greeks of the 2nd millennium BC had a writing system that fell out of use around 1100 BC, when their civilization was overrun by the Dorian invasions. Three or four centuries later the Phoenician writing system reached Greece. It is unclear where these signs, which are known from fragments of clay tablets, originally came from. One possibility is that they derive from certain Egyptian demotic signs.

What is certain is that the Phoenician alphabet only contained consonants. In other words, it consisted of

sounds or phonemes that only existed in the spoken
language when they were 'sounded', i.e. when they were
combined with vowels. Even today Semitic languages
such as Hebrew and Arabic are often written without

This bas-relief from
the palace of
Sargon II at Khorsabad
in Iraq shows
Phoenician merchants
transporting logs by
river. According to
Herodotus, who was
himself relaying an older
tradition, it was the
Phoenicians who
transmitted the art of
writing to the peoples
of the Mediterranean.

vowels. The Phoenicians were principally sailors and
merchants who travelled widely, trading their goods
with all the peoples of the eastern Mediterranean. Their
alphabet spread with them.

Two new alphabets come into existence: Aramaic and Hebrew. They are used in writing down the Old Testament

In about 800 BC, in the cities of modern Syria (then
called Aram), another alphabet was developed which was
in many aspects similar to that of the Phoenicians. This

was the Aramaic alphabet. Aramaic writing and language were to have a major impact on history, since it was in this language that several books of the Old Testament were written. The greater part of the Old Testament, however, has come down to us in Hebrew, of which the oldest known extant examples date to about 1000 BC.

In its early form Hebrew script did not include vowel sounds and was read, like Aramaic, from right to left. Ancient Hebrew is more or less the same language as that used today as the official language of the state of Israel. The 'square' script, as it is known, used for writing official documents, law scrolls and the like, has likewise changed little over the centuries, though a cursive script has evolved for daily use.

In more recent times Hebrew script came to be used to write Yiddish – a language composed mainly of Germanic and Slavic elements, quite unrelated to Hebrew and spoken by Central European Jews. Such a case illustrates the fact that a writing system can exist independently of the language that it was originally used to write.

Present-day Arabic and Hebrew scripts originate from the same source

The history of writing is decidedly a family history, for Arabic writing, like Hebrew, derives from the Phoenician alphabet. How did this come about? What

Hebrew square letter script, which records only the consonants, reads from right to left and seems to have developed from Aramaic. Below right: A fragment from the Passover ritual dating to the 16th century. Square letter Hebrew, slightly modified, is used in virtually the same way in Israel today.

These fragments of scrolls were discovered in 1947 in the caves at Kumran by the Dead Sea. In the spring of that year a shepherd of the Bedouin Ta'amireh tribe was hunting among the rocks for a straying sheep when he discovered the first cave of manuscripts. Parchment manuscripts had been hidden wrapped in linen, sealed with bitumen and placed in lidded clay jars. Now known as the Dead Sea Scrolls, they proved to contain biblical texts and commentaries written in Hebrew and Aramaic by members of the Essene sect.

were the contacts involved? We know very little, and the thread that links Phoenician writing with Arabic remains obscure. What does seem certain is that about the time of Christ the people of northern Arabia, called Nabateans, were already using a script that was neither Phoenician nor Arabic. Equally, it would seem to be an established fact that the first truly Arabic inscriptions date to AD 512–13.

Now it was in AD 622 that Mohammed, the prophet of Islam, fled from Mecca and took refuge at Medina. This date marks the beginning of the Hegira, i.e. the Muslim era. According to tradition, the first texts of

שֶׁנֶאֱמַר וְהִגַּדְתָּ לְבִנְךָ בַּיוֹם הַהוּא לֵאמֹר
בַּעֲבוּר זֶה עָשָׂה יְ"י לִי בְּצֵאתִי מִמִּצְרַיִם
וְהִגַּדְתָּ לְבִנְךָ יָכוֹל מֵרֹאשׁ חֹדֶשׁ תַּלְמוּד
לוֹמַר בַּיוֹם הַהוּא אִי בַּיוֹם הַהוּא יָכוֹל
מִבְּעוֹד יוֹם תַּלְמוּד לוֹמַר בַּעֲבוּר זֶה לֹא
אָמַרְתִּי אֶלָּא בְּשָׁעָה שֶׁמַּצָּה וּמָרוֹר מוּנָחִים
לְפָנֶיךָ

the Muslim holy book, the Koran, had been dictated to Mohammed by Allah some ten years earlier and were transcribed into Arabic script in about AD 650 so that even if the script slightly predated the emergence of Islam, its spread was due largely to the rapid expansion of Islam throughout the world.

And use of the Arabic script was even more widespread than that of the spoken language. Areas as far apart as North Africa, Asia Minor, India and parts of China were all subject to the Islamic conquest and all came to adopt its writing system. Indeed, had the peoples of the Western Christian world not driven the Saracens back in southern Europe, it is likely that Western Europeans would also be writing in Arabic characters today.

The Koran and the Bible: the very word 'writing' takes on religious connotations

When Christians speak of the 'Scriptures' (literally, 'writings'), they are of course referring to their holy books. In the same way, even the writing of the Koran is the 'writing of Allah', just as the hieroglyphs were the 'writing of the gods' in the eyes of the ancient Egyptians.

The words were to be revered whether or not they could be read and understood. Even today, in Koranic schools in parts of Asia and Africa, where other languages are spoken, the Koran is still studied in its original Arabic.

For these religious and other reasons Arabic writing developed to such an extent that it even came to be used to transcribe Persian. Persian, however, the language of

For Muslims, writing has a sacred character. The prophet Mohammed is believed to have recorded the word of Allah directly, with no other intermediary. In contrast to Persian manuscripts, where people are depicted (as shown opposite in a manuscript dating from the 16th century AD), texts of the Koran, the Muslim holy book, still respect today the religious principles of its first redactor, Uthman, the third caliph of Islam, who forbade the representation of Allah or Mohammed. Consequently, the letters themselves function as magnificent calligraphic decoration (left).

modern Iran, is an Indo-European language belonging to the same group as Latin and French, and has nothing whatever in common with Arabic, which is a Semitic language.

Over the centuries Arab calligraphy produces masterful creations of an extraordinary variety

As with Hebrew, Arabic is written and read from right to left and does not necessarily transcribe the vowels. The alphabet consists of eighteen letters, which, when counted up with their various marks and accents (used to indicate the vowels), comprise twenty-nine. In the cursive script the letters are joined together.

The true quality of the Arabic script, however, lies in its ability to take an infinite variety of forms. The Muslim religion forbids representation of the face of Allah or that of the prophet Mohammed, and, in certain sects, of any human beings; thus calligraphy has become the basic decorative element in mosques and on all other monuments. It forms the basis of an elaborate and imaginative ornamental art and has engendered a remarkable range of styles and concepts, ranging from the ancient Kufic (from the Iraqi town of Kufa) to the

This 19th-century calligram in Arabic script (below) is a 'bismillah', a calligraphic formula embodying the Arabic for 'In the name of Allah the merciful, the compassionate'. Within the body of the bird apears a Koranic verse celebrating paradise.

This detail from the decoration of the Dome of the Rock mosque in Jerusalem constitutes another type of 'bismillah'. Arab calligraphy is traditionally written in such letters within a mosaic square, usually blue in colour, which record the ninety-nine known names of Allah.

modern 'calligrams' of Hassan Massoudy (pp. 169–73). It is now known that in areas of southern Arabia, Ethiopia and even parts of the Sahara, alternative writing forms developed, undoubtedly also derived from Phoenician, although the majority of them have disappeared. The only ones

remaining are the Ethiopian script and Tifinagh, the script used by the Tuareg people, which is distinctive because of the highly geometric form of its characters (see p. 60). Tifinagh is highly unusual in the history of writing in being confined to women. Tuareg society is in fact matriarchal, and here, as elsewhere, literacy represents power.

Certain consonants from the Aramaic alphabet are borrowed by the Greeks to serve for vowels

All writing systems derived more or less directly from Phoenician script transcribe consonants only. In learning to read, the students of the ancient world simply had to memorize the vowel sounds. This was not a problem with the Semitic languages, as they had relatively few vowels, but it proved more awkward for languages such as Greek which had a high proportion of vowels.

In about the 8th century BC, while hieroglyphs were still current in Egypt and alphabetic scripts had been in use for more than two hundred years along the coast of Palestine, further north, in Greece, a totally different language was being spoken which could not be transcribed by any of the existing alphabetic systems.

The Greeks therefore had the idea of borrowing certain signs from the Aramaic alphabet to transcribe their vowel sounds, choosing those signs that represented consonants which did not exist in the Greek language. And so were born A ('alpha'), E ('epsilon'), O ('omicron') and Y ('upsilon'). I ('iota') was an innovation.

This outline summary ignores many of the

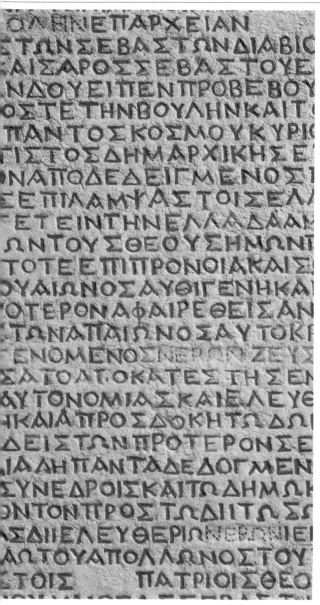

ΟΛΗΝΕΠΑΡΧΕΙΑΝ
ΤΩΝΣΕΒΑΣΤΩΝΔΙΑΒΙΟ
ΑΙΣΑΡΟΣΣΕΒΑΣΤΟΥΕ
ΝΔΟΥΕΙΠΕΝΠΡΟΒΕΒΟΥ
ΟΣΤΕΤΗΝΒΟΥΛΗΝΚΑΙΤ
ΠΑΝΤΟΣΚΟΣΜΟΥΚΥΡΙΟ
ΙΣΤΟΣΔΗΜΑΡΧΙΚΗΣΕ
ΝΑΠΟΔΕΔΕΙΓΜΕΝΟΣΤ
ΣΕΠΙΛΑΜΨΑΣΤΟΙΣΕΛ
ΕΤΕΙΝΤΗΝΕΛΛΑΔΑΑ
ΩΝΤΟΥΣΘΕΟΥΣΗΜΩΝΤ
ΤΟΤΕΕΠΙΠΡΟΝΟΙΑΚΑΙΣ
ΟΥΑΙΩΝΟΣΑΥΘΙΓΕΝΗΚΑ
ΟΤΕΡΟΝΑΦΑΙΡΕΘΕΙΣΑΝ
ΤΩΝΑΠΑΙΩΝΟΣΑΥΤΟΚΡ
ΕΝΟΜΕΝΟΣΝΕΡΩΝΖΕΥΣ
ΣΑΤΟΑΓΟΚΑΤΕΣΤΗΣΕΜ
ΑΥΤΟΝΟΜΙΑΣΚΑΙΕΛΕΥΘ
ΗΚΑΙΑΠΡΟΣΔΟΚΗΤΩΔΩΙ
ΔΕΙΣΤΩΝΠΡΟΤΕΡΟΝΣΕ
ΙΑΔΗΠΑΝΤΑΔΕΔΟΓΜΕΝ
ΣΥΝΕΔΡΟΙΣΚΑΙΤΩΔΗΜΩΙ
ΟΝΤΟΝΠΡΟΣΤΩΔΙΙΤΩΣ
ΣΔΙΙΕΛΕΥΘΕΡΙΩΝΕΡΩΝΙΕΙ
ΑΩΤΟΥΑΠΟΛΛΩΝΟΣΤΟΥ
ΤΟΙΣ   ΠΑΤΡΙΟΙΣΘΕΟ

This letter in Tifinagh (opposite, above), written by a young Tuareg woman to a Frenchman, bears witness to the longevity of an alphabet ultimately inspired by Phoenician.

This Greek translation of a discourse by the Emperor Nero on the freedom of the Greeks attests to the influence of Greek culture over Roman culture even after Greece had been annexed by the Roman empire in 146 BC. The Greek alphabet, with one or two alterations, was adopted by the founders of Rome. The letters A, B, E, Z, I, K, M, N, O, T, X and Y were all adopted almost unchanged. Greek characters were altered to form the letters G, L, S, P, R and D, while the letters V, F and Q, which had fallen into disuse in the Greek language, were resurrected by the Romans.

details of what was in fact a complex and lengthy process, but it is known for certain that by about the 5th century BC the Greek alphabet was in existence, consisting of twenty-four signs or letters, of which seventeen were consonants and seven vowels.

This alphabet could be written either in upper-case, 'capital', or lower-case letters. The upper case was most commonly used for inscriptions on stone; the lower case served for writing on papyrus or on wax tablets. The Greeks had invented a kind of writing tablet made

In 11th-century Italy it became fashionable to draw up official texts in Greek. In this illustrated treatise on fishing, hunting and farming, some of the letters are linked together by the ligatures that were so familiar to copyists of the Middle Ages.

of slate and covered with a layer of wax, on which pupils wrote their letters using a stylus or narrow stick. These exercises could then be erased by smoothing the soft surface of the wax.

Like the Egyptians, the Greeks also used a cheaper material – unglazed pottery, many examples of which have been recovered. The term for these, *ostraca*, reminds us of a particular aspect of Greek democracy:

ostracism. The names of undesirable individuals were written on fragments of pottery, which were then put into an urn. When an Athenian's name came up too often, he was exiled.

Our culture owes almost everything to Greek civilization, including the alphabet

Together with the Greek script, the Greeks also created, from the 5th and 4th centuries BC, one of the richest literatures of all time, including poetry, drama, epics, history and philosophy. We have inherited much of this literature, just as we have inherited the writing system in which it was recorded.

Greek was not only the forerunner of such complicated alphabets as Coptic, Armenian and Georgian; it was also the source of the Latin alphabet, that is to say our own. Or at least, so it would appear....

Here again, even though the main outline of the story is well established, the details are by no means straightforward.

We know that the Greeks were great sailors and that they sailed all over the Mediterranean. It therefore seems probable that they could have relayed their script to the Etruscans of Italy, who lived in the area that is now called Tuscany.

Thanks to Byzantine Christianity, Greek writing enjoyed a widespread influence and became the basis for four different families of writing: through Glagolitic to Cyrillic; through Armenian to Georgian; through Etruscan to Latin, and finally Coptic writing, the system used by the Christians of Egypt, the most recent form of the language of ancient Egypt. It existed side by side with Arabic; this manuscript of AD 1356, written in Coptic, includes an Arabic translation.

The 'Etruscan mystery' only serves to deepen the mystery of our Greek heritage

Creators of one of the richest civilizations of antiquity, the Etruscans left behind them in their elaborate underground tombs exquisite wall-paintings and statues of breathtaking beauty and sophistication. Numerous inscriptions have also been found, written in a script that bears a strong resemblance to that of the ancient Greeks. Unfortunately, the language of the Etruscans still remains so obscure that it is sometimes referred to as the 'Etruscan mystery'.

The Etruscan kings ruled Rome until the 4th century BC, when they were driven out by the people from the region of Latium. These conquering Latins, the future Romans, probably borrowed the Etruscan alphabet to write down their own tongue, Latin.

This is, however, only conjecture, since some authorities maintain that the Latin alphabet derived directly from the Greek without an Etruscan intermediary. Whatever the truth may prove to be, it is known for certain that around the 3rd century BC an alphabet consisting of nineteen letters evolved; X and Y were added much later, around the 1st century BC, in Cicero's time.

The Romans wrote in the same way as the Greeks, using upper-case letters for stone inscriptions and lower-case for other media such as papyrus or wax tablets.

From the 3rd century BC, lapidary script flourished on the monuments of the Roman empire. The effect of this monumental Roman 'quadrata' depends as much on the play of light and shadow as on the marks of the graver and chisel. Capital letters were always used. The 'quadrata' remains to this day the prototype for all monumental inscriptions.

What is the origin of the Etruscan alphabet whose letters can be seen on this vase (left)? Does it derive from the alphabet of Cumae, a Greek colony in Campania, or from the Boeotian Greek model? The discovery of an identical script, dating to the 6th century, on the island of Lemnos has given new impetus to the debate; it could be the result of an Etruscan import into the Aegean.

ROMVLVS MARTIS
FILIVS VRBEM ROMAM
CONDIDIT ET REGNAVIT ANNOS
DVODEQVADRAGINTA ISQVE
PRIMVS DVX DVCE HOSTIVM
ACRONE REGE CAENINENSIVM
INTERFECTO SPOLIA OPIMA
IOVI FERETRIO CONSECRAVIT
RECEPTVSQVE IN DEORVM
NVMERVM QVIRINVS
APPELLATVS EST

Inscriptions on stone required highly detailed preparations. Obviously, it was necessary to calculate in advance the size of the letters, in terms of the number of words in the inscription and the amount of space available. The engraver would therefore have begun

This Pompeian couple is famous. The woman, who is probably the wife of Terentius Neo, is seen holding a stylus and a wax tablet. Terentius Neo himself is holding a roll of papyrus, or *volumen*, which was written on with a brush. It was, however, the stylus (an instrument that had been used for centuries in various forms) that the Romans used most frequently in their writing. It is thought that Tiro, Nero's secretary, used a stylus and wax tablets to transcribe the speeches of the great orator. One end of the bronze stylus was pointed and produced an even line when writing. The other was flattened like a spatula and would have been used for erasing and smoothing the surface for re-use.

his task by measuring out his text, probably on a roll of papyrus. Then he would have drawn lines on the stone with chalk to indicate the positions of the tops and bottoms of the letters, much in the way that signwriters do today. After this the letters would have been drawn using charcoal, and then painted. Only at this point could the actual engraving process begin.

The 2nd and 3rd centuries AD saw the appearance of a new, popular writing system and 'uncial' writing, which were to spread to all the regions of Europe that were dominated by the Romans, and where Latin was written, up to about AD 1000.

Surprisingly, it appears that Indian scripts can probably claim the same origins as our own alphabet

Indian writing first appeared in the 3rd century BC, when the edicts of the great ruler Asoka (272–231) were

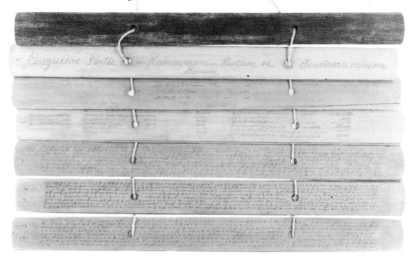

committed to stone. Following these inscriptions, two principal writing systems appear in the Indian subcontinent: Kharosthi and Brahmi – not counting the many variants used to transcribe the multiplicity of languages spoken in that vast country.

Brahmi is at the root of the Devanagari script used to record Sanskrit, the holy language of much of India, which gradually gave way to vernacular speech. Brahmi also lies behind one of the most widespread modern languages, Hindi. A totally alphabetic system, Brahmi script contains both consonants and vowels. This has led scholars to conclude that these scripts did not originate locally but can ultimately be traced back to the Phoenician alphabet.

It is certainly true that major trade routes existed between India, and in particular the Indus valley, and the eastern Mediterranean, so there were many

On this fragment of a Tamil book found in southern India one can read part of the epic *Kambaramayanam*. Tamil writing, a variant of Brahmi, notates both consonants and vowels. The most interesting aspect of this book is the medium on which it is written: bamboo strips, threaded together so that they can be folded up over each other or folded out flat in order to be read.

opportunities for contact with Arabia, the Phoenician coast and even Greece. There was also the extraordinary expedition made by Alexander the Great along the banks of the river Indus in 326 BC. And, finally, one must not forget the fact that some of the Indian languages, in particular Sanskrit, are themselves Indo-European languages. There are therefore several arguments to support the theory of a common origin for all these scripts.

As early as the 4th century BC the Indians are already highly skilled grammarians

In the 4th century BC Panini, an Indian born in Salatura and considered to be the first grammarian, was able to describe the exact functions of the consonants and vowels in Sanskrit, the Indian 'writing of the gods'.

Mongol manuscript of the 17th century.

The text on this carved stone, below, found in Nepal, is a series of Buddhist prayers. The writing is Tibetan, which derives from Devanagari.

This is not so surprising in view of the fact that Indian scripts are integrally alphabetic and show a highly structured phonetic system.

The main languages in India (which are usually read from left to right) contain a principal vowel: 'a'. Words are normally arranged around a 'power', a form of large horizontal bar that links all the letters to each other above an imaginary line. This particular form of script lends them a peculiarly fluid beauty.

The scripts used in present-day Tibet and other southeast Asian countries – Laos, Thailand, Kampuchea (Cambodia) and Burma – are all modelled on the Indian scripts, although the precise details of their evolution are complicated.

The Vietnamese writing system does not belong to the same family as these scripts. Here the Latin alphabet was introduced in the 17th and 18th centuries by proselytizing Portuguese Jesuits, who found that northern and southern Vietnam used different writing systems and saw that it would be easier to convert the people if they could all read the same script.

In order to do this they invented a system for transcribing the Vietnamese tongue called 'chu-quôc-ngu' (which means 'characters of the language of the country'), or more simply 'quôc-ngu'. Since the Latin characters could reproduce the sounds of the Vietnamese language only imperfectly, a number of dots and accents, more accurately called diacriticals, were added to the script.

This Indian manuscript, dating to the 19th century, is written in Nagari. 'Nagari' means 'from the town' in Sanskrit, and 'Devanagari' means 'god of the town'.

Contrary to what most Westerners assume, literacy is far from being universal

At the time of Christ various writing systems were in existence in various parts of the world, but not everywhere by any means. Even today there are still many areas where large numbers of people do not know how to write. Linguists have documented some three thousand different languages in use throughout the world, but of these only about a hundred are normally written down. It must also be remembered that one adult in two cannot, or can only just, write.

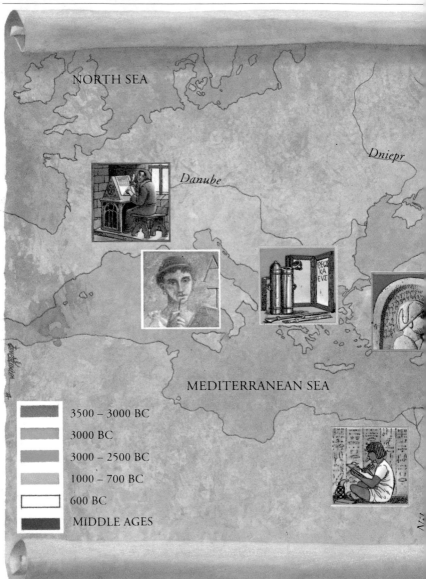

NORTH SEA

Dniepr

Danube

MEDITERRANEAN SEA

3500 – 3000 BC
3000 BC
3000 – 2500 BC
1000 – 700 BC
600 BC
MIDDLE AGES

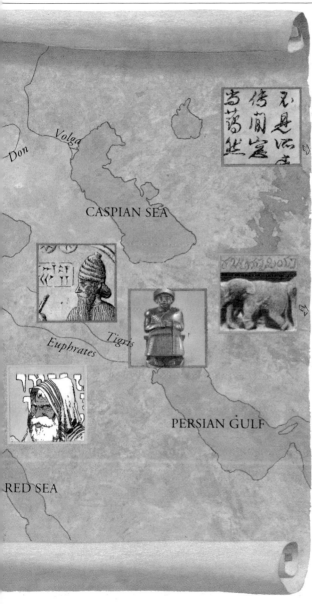

The dates given below are schematic. In reality the appearance of different forms of writing often overlapped.

3500 – 3000 BC
The Uruk civilization dawns in Sumer. Pictograms appear for keeping accounts. In China, writing develops from pictograms to ideograms and phonograms.

3000 BC
India sees a parallel development of writing. The first early writing appears on stone and copper tablets.

3000 – 2500 BC
Hieroglyphs are being developed on the banks of the Nile.

1000 – 700 BC
The Phoenician alphabet paves the way for Greek and its modern alphabet, which includes vowels. Moving east, the Arameans provide the forerunners for the Hebrew and Arabic scripts.

600 BC
Greeks as well as Etruscans begin to settle in Rome. Latin appears for the first time on the 'Black Stone' of the Forum.

Middle Ages
Carolingian, Gothic and humanist scripts record Latin in Western Europe, while Cyrillic, derived from Greek, develops further east.

Along with their civilization, the Romans left us their language, Latin, and, with their language, their writing system. Five centuries after the fall of the Roman empire, Charlemagne proclaimed Christianity the heir to Roman civilization. He set to work to revive a knowledge and a culture that had been on the point of disappearing in a Europe long subjugated by the Barbarians.

CHAPTER 4

FROM COPYISTS TO PRINTERS

In the Middle Ages a form of sacred writing became established in the monasteries, which was beautifully designed and executed, reflecting the serenity both of those who created it and the setting in which they worked.

For centuries any Gaul or Briton who could write, wrote Latin, and when Christianity began to spread, the writing and copying of texts continued to be carried on in Latin.

The Oaths of Strasbourg, in 842, mark the first appearance of a vernacular language in an official document. In this treaty, which was written in both Old German and Old French, two of the grandsons of Charlemagne – Charles the Bald and Louis the German – swore allegiance against the third grandson, Lothar. However, it was to be a long time before Old French writing made more than very rare appearances compared to Latin.

Secular copyists sometimes allowed themselves charming indulgences. This mid-15th-century collection of love songs has been bound into a heart-shaped book.

For more than a thousand years writing skills are virtually the monopoly of monks

Very few lay individuals mastered the art of writing. Charlemagne, undoubtedly the most powerful man in Western Europe at the time, was illiterate. He signed royal commands with a cross, which he inserted into the loops of the signature prepared for him by one of his scribes.

Unlike the Mesopotamian and Egyptian scribes, the monks who were trained as copyists in Europe in the Middle Ages were neither creative writers nor men of power; they wrote, but they did not compose. The creative aspects of their work lay in a different area, that of calligraphy. Particularly from the time of Charlemagne onwards, they raised the writing of letters to the level of an art form, creating exquisite illuminated manuscripts – meaning literally, written by hand – decorated with beautiful handwriting and ornament, which were to become the first books.

The early scribes, for example those who copied biblical texts, wrote on rolls of papyrus, called *volumen* in Latin. However, these *volumen* were far from ideal;

The composition of an illuminated letter went through several stages. First, all its elements (the letter itself, the background and figures) were sketched out in pencil; then the drawing was worked over using ink, before the application of gilding and the insertion of touches of colour, interwoven and underlined with touches of shadow. The lavishly employed red colour was obtained by mixing minium (red lead) with either egg white or yolk, which gave it a lustrous chestnut colour. The terms 'miniature' and 'miniaturist' derive from this use of minium.

Astronomical calligrams

This manuscript,
entitled *Phenomena*,
is a Carolingian version
of a poem by the Greek
author Aratus, who lived
in Asia Minor around
300 BC. It is an
astronomical text which
enumerates the celestial
constellations, giving
their respective positions
and their relative
brightness, as well as
their relation to the
twelve signs of the
zodiac. It was translated
by Cicero in his youth.
Hugo Grotius finished
the translation, which
had remained
incomplete, with verses
of his own devising.
Finally, Julius Hyginus
added the curious
figures filled by *capitalis
rustica*, which the Saxon
artist usually drew in red
minium or in brown, in
bluish hues or different
shades of grey.

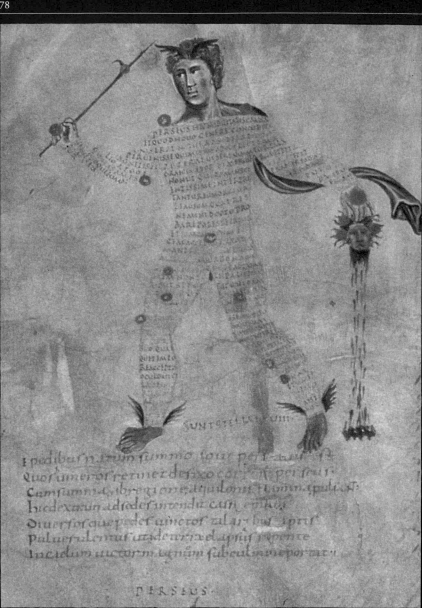

SVNT OTELLA XV IIII

E pedibus in cuin summo Iovis perseus it
Quos umeros retinet deixo corpore perseus
Cumsumma libra oreat quidonat tunc epula est
hic dexterin adicder intendit caput eriuts
Diuersoaque pedes umeros talaribus apris
Paluerulentus ut deterrix elapius repente
Incidium auctorum tignum subeubsumeportat

PERSEVS

The twenty-five leaves of the *Phenomena* manuscript present a series of mythological figures, such as Perseus (far left), fabulous animals like the Hydra, birds and fish, including an eagle, a dolphin and a dog, and objects, such as a ship, a lyre, the delta sign, and also the planets. Although technically it would be anachronistic to call these 'calligrams' (since the French poet Guillaume Apollinaire only invented the term a thousand years later), that is effectively what they are; the texts express through their shapes the outline of animate or inanimate objects. These are then given 'bodies' of text, somewhat like the famous collages of Georges Braque and Pablo Picasso. To superimpose an image on a text is today a commonplace of advertising. Are modern designers aware that the technique was already in use in manuscript illumination a thousand years ago?

papyrus was costly and fragile, and only one side of the sheet could be used. Furthermore, it was awkward to handle, and referring to texts written on rolls of papyrus was no easy matter.

Had parchment not been invented, the art of illumination would never have reached such heights

The introduction of a new medium, parchment, was completely to alter the art of writing. Parchment appears to have originated at Pergamon, in Asia Minor. The word parchment comes from the Greek *pergamene*, meaning skin 'from Pergamon'. In the 2nd century BC Egypt had refused to supply its rival Pergamon with the papyrus essential for writing, so the scribes of Asia Minor had to resort to an alternative material: leather. They therefore lay claim to the invention of parchment. In fact it would seem that animal skin had been used at an earlier date by the Egyptians themselves.

Parchment is usually made from either sheepskin, calfskin or goatskin, although gazelle, antelope and even ostrich skins are known to have been used as the base material. Sheepskin and calfskin have the advantage over the others that both sides of the sheet can be written on.

Vellum is high quality parchment made by using the

In the preparation of parchment, burnishing was the most crucial stage. The outer surface of the skin, where the fibres were more tightly packed and could better withstand scraping by the blade, was chosen for preference. The internal surface had the disadvantage that it tended to become fluffy under the knife or pumice stone.

This detail from an 18th-century Dutch painting encapsulates centuries of writing history. It depicts the manuscript of an anonymous copyist of the Middle Ages, who is piously transcribing the Bible of Saint Jerome, Father and Doctor of the Church, who revised the Holy Writ in the 4th century and translated it from Hebrew, Aramaic and Greek into Latin. The righthand page of the manuscript shows an illuminated capital, while that on the left has a full-page illustration of Christ in Majesty.

skins of either very young calves or even stillborn animals. Its name comes from the Old French *velin,* meaning 'calf'. Its principal quality is that it does not soak up ink or paint and so preserves the original colours better. This is why the most beautiful illuminations were done on vellum.

Cumbersome papyrus gives way to sheets of parchment bound together as a 'codex'; thus the book proper is born

To make parchment, the hides were soaked in a lime bath, then scrubbed and cleansed of all traces of flesh and hair. Before being laid out to dry on grids, they were dusted with plaster to absorb any remaining grease. After this they were again scraped down.

It was crucial that the tanning process was perfectly carried out, otherwise the parchment retained an intolerable smell. The copyist's first task was to smooth the sheets of parchment using a knifeblade or pumice stone to remove any marks or bumps, and to produce a lightly grained, polished surface that would absorb the ink without allowing it to spread.

The appearance of parchment brought two distinct advances: first, it allowed the goose quill to be used, an implement that offered vastly more potential than the somewhat limited reed-brush; second, the sheets could be folded and sewn together in the manner of the Roman 'codex'; forerunners of our books, these were made up of leaves that were specially folded and then bound together.

A goose feather, selected from among the five best wing quills of a large fowl, preferably from the left wing, was allowed to soak for several hours in order to soften it; once it had been dried and hardened in hot sand, it could be cut with a knife (below left).

From the 9th or 10th century each abbey and monastery has its own scriptorium

The scriptorium, where manuscripts were copied, decorated and bound, was usually located near the library. It could either be a separate room, called the 'warming room' (because it was the only heated room in the monastery), or a collection of individual cells, depending on the religious order. In the poorest monasteries the scriptorium would often be located in the cloisters.

Each copyist had his or her own seat, despite the fact that a certain amount of the work would have been done standing, and a pivoting, double-sided desk for use when the copyist needed to see two manuscripts at once. The *scriptores*, as they were known, wrote using goose-quill pens which were cut to different shapes depending on the style of writing to be

produced. These had to be re-trimmed regularly and required frequent re-filling with ink. Each copyist was able to cover on average about four leaves per day, one leaf of parchment being equivalent to a sheet 35–50 cm tall by 25–30 cm wide.

Flawless organization and a rigorous division of labour lie at the root of manuscript production

The painstaking task of copying was only interrupted by the routine of daily prayers. If one is to judge from the spelling errors and disparities in graphic technique that can be found within the same manuscript, it would appear that the copyists wrote from dictation, and that several copyists worked on the same book. This work was often done in collaboration with nuns, since by the Middle Ages mixed communities were becoming more common.

"If you do not know what writing is, you may think it is not especially difficult.... Let me tell you that it is an arduous task: it destroys your eyesight, bends your spine, squeezes your stomach and your sides, pinches your lower back and makes your whole body ache.... Like the sailor arriving at the port, so the writer rejoices on arriving at the last line. *De gratias semper.***"**

Colophon of a 12th-century Beatus manuscript from Silos

Novices, apprentices and beginners were given the task of marking the lines – the 'guidelines' – which the copyists then used to align the letters. There are many manuscripts where the guidelines have not been erased. Beginners were also given less intricate work, of which there was a considerable amount, since the copying of manuscripts represented an important source of income for the monasteries.

Calligraphers, illuminators, miniaturists and binders: the monastic copyists become artists, and their works, masterpieces

The best calligraphers were chosen for highly prestigious tasks, usually for commissions from members of the nobility or higher clergy. The talent of these anonymous artists was, however, not always compatible with the golden monastic rule of humility, and some monks were unable to escape the temptations of vanity, proudly

Beneath the lines of writing on the parchment can be seen the guidelines used by the copyist when positioning his letters. The instrument he holds in his right hand is for outlining the script. Some writing specialists are able to distinguish, from the writing in a given manuscript, whether the scribe was left- or right-handed, from his *ductus*, the way he linked the letters, which was determined by the cut of his quill pen.

"He [the Carthusian copyist] should be given an ink well, quill pens, chalk, two pumice stones, two horns, a small knife, two razors for scraping the parchment, one ordinary stylus and one finer one, a lead pencil, a ruler, some writing tablets and a stylet."

Guignes de Chartreux
Customs

This 11th-century writing tablet contains a kind of pencil box, in which goose quills were kept. Its cover has been richly decorated.

setting their names to works that they justifiably held to be masterpieces. When this happened, and a monk made an ostentatious parade of his talents, he was obliged to stop working and could only begin again when he had accepted that his art was exercised solely in the service of God and his religious order.

Decorative work was the preserve of the illuminators and the miniaturists. These specialists were highly gifted artists, capable of producing not only the gilded dropped initials that began every paragraph and chapter, but also the drawings of flowers, people and the countryside in the vibrantly coloured miniatures that illustrate the finest of these books. The motif was first outlined using a stylus, and then the details were added with a goose-quill pen and ink, and when necessary a pair of compasses, a ruler and a set-square. Even the colour outlines were done with a pen, and it was only the final infilling that was done using a fine brush.

If a monastery could not find a sufficiently skilled artist for a specific task among its own community it would hire the services of a qualified secular artist. They would also call on the *illigator liborum*, the bookbinder, who was responsible for making the leather book cover and the clasp, which were often very beautifully worked.

These initials from German manuscripts, dating to the middle of the 13th century, portray different stages in the making of a book: the delivery of the parchment to a monk; the marking of the lines by the scribe; painting a portrait; and the trimming of the sheets of vellum.

This 7th-century manuscript, the *Treatise of Saint Hilary*, is written in uncial.

Until the reign of Charlemagne, the copyists enjoy a certain freedom in their choice of characters

At first the monks used all the letters of the Roman period: the 'cursive upper case', also referred to as the 'uncial', the 'semi-uncial', a smaller and rounder form, and also the 'capital', the square upper case used in monumental inscriptions, and sometimes also a less sophisticated capital, used in votive monumental inscriptions – the 'rustic'.

Until the invention of printing, the uncial referred to the rounded letters written with a pen as opposed to the square letter forms of engraved monumental inscriptions.

Shortly after the beginning of Charlemagne's reign in 768, a totally new script appeared, the 'Carolingian', apparently inspired by the form of the semi-uncial letter. This script, with its clarity and formal beauty, became widespread throughout Western medieval Europe for many centuries.

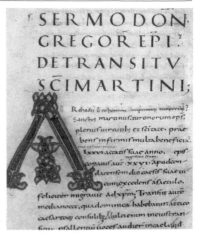

In Carolingian script the capital letters are very neatly and regularly formed, and the lower-case letters are smaller and finer than the uncials. This Latin manuscript of Sulpicius Severus is a *Life of Saint Martin* dating to the end of the 9th century. The relative severity of the decorated initial letter is typical of manuscripts of this period.

The reign of Charlemagne also witnessed an enormous preoccupation with textual accuracy. With the passing of time innumerable errors had crept into the manuscripts. The ignorance or negligence of monks had allowed these changes to be perpetuated, sometimes to such an extent that the whole meaning of a passage was altered. Charlemagne decided to remedy this by ordering the creation of new copies, done with the greatest care, from the best authenticated sources. Carolingian manuscripts that were standardized in this way are marked *ex authentico libro*, guaranteeing a perfect transcription of the original.

The secularization of writing gives rise to a new class of artisan

Towards the end of the 12th century the quasi-monopoly of the church over teaching began to weaken, and the secular scribes, who were collaborating with the monks, began to organize themselves into guilds and workshops. They drafted official documents for the new merchant bourgeoisie and they also wrote books.

Until then the issuing of books had been the exclusive domain of the nobility and the clergy; luxury works for the former, and missals and theological manuals for the

The illuminator (who was often a layman, as in this case) receives a visit from a noble patron in his workshop. The tools of his trade are ranged in front of him. Most of the touches of gold decoration in the illuminations were done by attaching very fine gold leaf to a coating made of a mixture of plaster, sugar and lead, which was applied lightly to the page and dried slightly on the surface. The coating had to remain sufficiently flexible to bend with the page without cracking, and to flow freely from a pen, when mixed with water and egg white.

latter comprised the total output of book production. This output was now expanded with new works; treatises on philosophy, logic, mathematics and astronomy all began to appear, while authors such as Dante began to write in their own tongue, thus reaching a much wider public, who were educated, although unable to read Latin. For the first time the middle classes had access to literature and to books.

The *Romaunt de la Rose* (opposite) was begun by Guillaume de Loris and continued by Jean de Meung. The vignette in the lefthand column represents the writer of the second part of the story.

It soon becomes difficult for the artisans to satisfy the demand

In order to cope with this new demand, the number of scribal workshops increased, and production diversified. From now on, books of all sorts appeared – cookery books, educational books, medical manuals, books on astronomy and even novels. Tales of courtly love, such as the *Song of Roland*, were much sought-after. The

client chose the calligraphic style and the type of illustration by visiting different workshops, or more commonly by dealing with a book supplier who acted as an intermediary.

In the 12th and 13th centuries guilds and fraternities grow up around the universities

Gradually, a student element was added to the ever-increasing clientele of well-to-do merchants. The rise of secular universities provided an important source of work for copyists in the reproduction of authorized texts. In fact, only the most fortunate students were able to call upon the professionals; the others had to hire *exemplaria* from registered booksellers and copy them themselves, word by word.

With the vast increase in work, the artisans began increasingly to specialize, and to form fraternities, who were careful to protect their rights and the secrets of their techniques. Apprenticeship was also very strictly controlled. Like their religious counterparts, aspiring calligraphers had to begin with the most menial tasks, sketching the lines or grinding the colours. A seven-year period was held to be the minimum length of time necessary for apprenticeship, of which the last year was partly devoted to the production of a 'masterpiece', which would be judged by the chief craftsman and fellow artisans. If the work was adjudged worthy of the guild, the apprentice was awarded the title of independent scribe and obtained the right to set up his own business, on condition that he moved away from the area of his master's workshop, in order to avoid competition.

Correction of manuscripts gives rise to somewhat whimsical additions

According to John Dreyfus, a historian of book production, the apprentices' code strongly recommended that student scribes should retain a steady hand, not only by avoiding all excesses of good food and drink, but also by abstaining from too frequent contact with women and from heavy work.

This fragment from the *Reform of the Order of St Benedict* is written in Gothic script, a sharply angular style of writing that appeared in the 13th century.

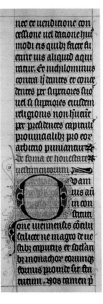

The knife and the ruler (right) were among the more essential tools for a copyist.

Obviously, a scribe had to be able to adapt to all writing styles and to be able to calligraph any text. But for all his flexibility, he was not infallible. The workshops often appointed a reader, who would mark any error he found in the margin along with the necessary correction. If the error was small the scribe would scrape the parchment and then write over the clean surface. If a whole word was missing which could not be inserted, he could write it in the margin and then draw a finger to indicate its correct position in the text. When it was a question of complete lines or paragraphs that had been omitted, however, the scribe would correct the omission by writing the text at the bottom of the page for the illustrator to frame and add illustrations of people appearing to climb up to the desired position.

Despite the fact that the production of books continued to increase, and that the scribal fraternity insisted on the highest standards, so that some of the works produced were truly magnificent, the artists and artisans involved had no social status and were only just able to earn a living. Sometimes the most gifted of the scribes and artists would adopt the religious life simply

in order to be able to write without having to worry about the material aspects of daily life.

Reflecting cultural changes, Gothic letters give way to humanist script

Changes in the production of manuscripts were naturally accompanied by changes in the characters used; copyists tended towards the use of letter forms of

The cutting of the quill was done in several stages.

(1) Cutting the end of the quill at an angle.

(2) Making a slit in the middle of the tip.

(3) Making the nib by cutting the sides away evenly.

(4) If the underneath of the nib was too concave, it was flattened by cutting the tip.

(5) To shape the nib, the point was placed on a smooth, hard surface.

German provenance, called 'Gothic'. This was in fact as much for material as for cultural reasons. The Gothic letters were narrower than the 'Carolingian', giving the scribe more space on the parchment. Furthermore, quills now began to be cut with a bevelled edge, forcing the scribes to hold the quill to one side, rather than flat, a technique that was perfectly suited to this angular, broken script. This was the time when 'Gothic' architecture began to appear, and analogies can be drawn between the intersecting vaults and pointed arches of Gothic windows and the forms of Gothic writing.

From the 14th to 15th centuries in Italy, however, a writing style appeared that completely rejected Gothic forms. It was rounder and broader, and took the significant name of 'humanist' script. This style of lettering had become very widely used, when an event took place that was to have an incalculable effect on European culture: the invention of the letter press, a printing process using movable letters.

This Italian manuscript in Latin dates from 1458, the dawn of humanism.

Johannes Gutenberg's contemporaries have no idea of the extent of his revolution in book production

The Chinese had been using movable characters since the 11th century AD. The screw press had also been known for centuries and had been used before Gutenberg's time – for pressing grapes, 'surfacing' paper and impressing patterns on textiles. At the beginning of the 15th century words carved on wooden blocks were being printed on paper to accompany pictures of saints or biblical scenes. But these prints were obtained by placing the sheet on the block of wood and rubbing the back of it. Johannes Gutenberg of Mainz was the first to mechanize printing in *c.* 1447, and Peter Schoeffer, a friend of Gutenberg's, discovered a method for casting letters, especially those with asymmetrical shapes, by using an alloy of lead and antimony.

In this 15th-century printing workshop each man has his task. On the right the master printer stands by the press, which an apprentice is supplying with paper. The printed sheets are hung up to dry above them. On the far left, two compositors are arranging the type, reading from the text laid out in front of them, while in the foreground a worker replaces the used type in its cases, and behind him a proof-reader checks the first proofs. In the background a man is inking the printing blocks using leather stamps covered with felt. Similar cone-shaped stamps can also be seen next to the Gutenberg press (far left), rebuilt in the last century at Leipzig.

Initially, printing appeared much more like an extension of handwriting than the total change that we, with the benefit of hindsight, can see that it was. The printer's main purpose was to set himself up as a rival to the scribe, and to succeed in producing volumes that were as luxurious as the calligraphers' works.

It is not known for certain whether Gutenberg was solely responsible for the printing of his Latin bible in 1450. This bible is still heavily influenced by the medieval spirit; it is richly illuminated and uses Gothic characters. It is known as the 'Thirty-six line' Bible (there were thirty-six lines per column) to distinguish it from the 642-page, so-called Mazarin Bible, printed in 1455, which had forty-two lines per column. These two works belong to what is conventionally called the *incunabulum* ('cradle' in Latin), i.e. books printed before 1500. Also included are the *Psalterium* of 1457 and the first non-religious work, Cicero's *De Officiis*, of 1465. William Caxton set up the first English press in 1476, and the first book to be printed in England was *The Dictes or Sayinges of the Philosophers* of 1477.

For this reason large areas of the printed page were left blank to be decorated afterwards by an illuminator, and the printer endeavoured to produce a page that was as close in appearance as possible to the handwritten page.

In order to do this, extremely elaborate capital letters were created, and the characters and signs multiplied; the printer even went so far as to join some of the characters together as if they had been written by a quill pen. Dreyfus writes 'The first printed book had to be just as fine, in both concept and execution, as the handwritten books with which it would be compared. The splendour of the Gutenberg Bible printed in 1450 owes much to the handwriting and decoration of the hand-produced contemporary bibles.'

Nevertheless, printing did not immediately take the place of writing. Its progress depended on the solution of many difficult technical problems.

The slow and laborious process of producing the written word is greatly speeded up with the introduction of paper

Gutenberg was well aware of all the advantages of paper, a material that had long been in use in China.

It is not known exactly when the Chinese invented paper, but it was probably in the 2nd century AD. We know that they experimented with various different materials before finding that flax fibres, frequently derived from recycled rags, produced the best quality. First reduced by soaking, then washed and crushed, flax fibre produced a pulp from which paper could be made by adding water and starch.

The Chinese kept this process a closely guarded secret and would not surrender it to their Mongolian conquerors until the 8th century. The latter then passed it on to the Persians at Samarkand, who taught the Arab merchants; they in turn brought it to Spain and Sicily. In the 13th century major paper manufacturing centres were set up in Europe. With the exception of one or two improvements, the method of manufacture was the same as that initiated by the Chinese.

The story that begins now is no longer just the story of writing, but also that of typography, of printing and of the development of book production.

Johannes Gänsefleisch (1397–1468), known as Gutenberg, established himself in Mainz after spending eight years in Strasbourg. He borrowed money from the banker Johann Fust, but soon found himself unable to repay him. In 1455 the banker confiscated all Gutenberg's material, which he then hired back to him. When the first work bearing the colophon of a printer appeared in 1457 it was Fust's name that it bore. Gutenberg himself died a decade later, a ruined man.

With the success of Gutenberg's press, it seemed likely that writing by hand would become a thing of the past. Far from it. Thanks to printing, the literary world expanded to reach ever greater proportions, while the quill pen remained the indispensable tool for recording thought.

CHAPTER 5
MEN OF
THE BOOK

The hand-held pen illustrated in the *Encyclopédie* of Denis Diderot and Jean D'Alembert (right) and the hand-turned press in Bernardo Cennini's workshop (left). In the 17th century the rapid development of the latter gave new impetus to the former. The act of writing was from now on linked to that of printing.

One major result of the extraordinary development
of printing and the vast increase in the number of books,
both in Europe and throughout the rest of the world,
was the gradual spread of the knowledge and use of
written languages. Knowing the written form of a
language held a certain power, just as it had done for
early scribes. As Jean-Paul Sartre said in *Les Mots*
('*Words*'), it is by mastering writing that we gain 'the
means to conquer the world'.

History has not preserved the name of the Chinese
Gutenberg, though it should have done so. For it is in
faraway China that scholars locate the production of the
first book printed with movable metal letters, in 1390.
How this invention arrived in Europe is obscure.
All that is known is that from 1462 onwards the use
of the Mainz printing press developed by Gutenberg,
Fust and Schoeffer spread throughout Europe.

From the beginning of the 16th century printing houses grow up, combining the talents of engravers, type-casters and compositors

In Venice Aldus Manutius (1449–1515) endeavoured
to produce the most beautiful script possible employing
metal letters. He invented the 'lettera antica', which was
to be used in Europe throughout the 16th century. This
script became a model for many engravers. Seeking to
reproduce handwriting, Aldus was also inspired by the
writing of Petrarch to create 'Aldine', or 'italic', an
elegant, slanting cursive script. Luca Paccioli's *De Divina
Proportione* (1509) attempted to create a script by
reducing the proportions of the human body to
geometric shapes, in the style of drawings by the
Renaissance artist Leonardo da Vinci.

During the early 16th century the initiative shifted
from Italy to France, where in 1530 the works of
Geoffroy Tory had considerable impact on printing.
An engraver and compositor, as well as an ardent
admirer of Leonardo da Vinci, Tory worked in the same
direction as Paccioli, creating the 'Champ-Fleury' style.
He was soon appointed designer to Simon de Colines,

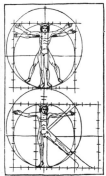

Hardly had print escaped from the rigid Gothic block-letter of Gutenberg, than it was confined in the new rationalism of Renaissance humanism. And if artists such as Leonardo da Vinci and Albrecht Dürer failed to establish a canon of aesthetic perfection for art in general, the type-casters came very close to it in the context of printing. Above: Illustrations from Geoffroy Tory's 1529 treatise on writing, *Champ-Fleury*.

With the co-operation of the engraver Francesco Griffo, Aldus Manutius created a slanting font called 'Aldine', or more commonly 'italic'. All slanted letters were from then on referred to as 'italic'. The sign of this great Venetian founder of an entire dynasty of printers is shown left.

a printer located in the Rue de la Montagne-Sainte-Geneviève in Paris, under the sign of the Golden Sun.

Simon de Colines, whose type was derived from the 'lettera antica', set himself the task of creating and engraving a Greek font. His work was to be used, some ten years later, in 1540–1, in the design of the famous 'Grecs du roi', which Claude Garamond engraved following the models provided by the Cretan calligrapher Angel Vergèce. These fonts, commissioned by François I, are now kept at the Imprimerie Nationale in Paris, and were designated *monuments historiques* in 1946. After this, Garamond cast a set of Roman characters, inspired by those of Tory, which were destined to become the aristocrats (*lettres de noblesse*) of the typographical world; the 'Roman Garamond' is indeed an alphabet that exhibits, according to the 'Champ-Fleury' formula, 'the art and the science of the fitting and true proportions of letters'.

In France Estienne, and in Holland Plantin and Elzevir foreshadow the manufacturing press

During the reign of François I, a humanist king with a great love of literature, a dynasty of creators of characters, the Estiennes, emerged. In spite of the king's support, they were forced to flee to Geneva, where Martin Luther was making use of the Gothic script to broadcast the ideas of the Reformation among the people, and from the end of the 16th century they turned that town into the major European publishing centre. Until the mid-18th century the Estiennes – consecutively Henri I, Robert, Charles, Henri II, Paul and Antoine – brought fame to a profession that combined the scholarly translation of ancient works, the composition of new works and the creation of new typefaces.

Further north, in Holland, Christophe Plantin, a Frenchman who had become a citizen of Antwerp and a bookbinder appointed chief typographer to Philip II of Spain, was managing with real genius to exploit the full potential of the printing press; he had sixteen presses functioning at once in his workshop. In thirty-four years Plantin published over fifteen hundred works, one of which was the famous polyglot bible, compiled under the supervision of the Spanish humanist Arias Montanus. Together with the Elzevir dynasty, established at Leiden, which produced books in compactly set type on very fine Angoulême paper, Plantin was the last of the great publishers of the Renaissance and the forerunner of industrial printers.

Robert Estienne, printer to the king in Hebrew, Latin and Greek from 1540. A brilliant humanist and great publisher, he produced bibles, psalters and numerous ancient authors under the sign of the olive tree, the family emblem. In 1539 he compiled a Latin–French dictionary. Although he was a friend of François I, the king could not protect him from the attacks of the Sorbonne, which forced him into exile.

With the expansion of printing, the process of bookbinding, until then a task confined to monks, became more practical and public. By the 16th century the bookbinder was an artisan who ran a prosperous business (left), and as the skill became more secularized, the bookbinders formed guilds. The introduction of machinery at the end of the 18th century, and the rapid growth in book production during the 19th century, did much to injure the art of the craftsman in binding. Today it is rare to find a hand-made binding created especially for the book it contains.

A pocket-sized format facilitates the spread of radical ideas

At the end of the 16th century, as the Counter-Reformation and the Inquisition gained power and suppressed many new ideas, Protestant Holland became a safe-house for the publishing fraternity in Europe. Absolute monarchy was ill-suited to these men of letters, who after 1550 gave up Latin, preferring to publish the Greek and Latin classics in their own national languages.

The memory of the martyred publisher from Lyons, Etienne Dolet, was still fresh in their minds. Dolet's editions of the works of François Rabelais, Clément Marot, and especially the *Enchiridion Militis Christiani* of Erasmus had aroused the wrath of the Inquisition, and he was burned at the stake in Paris on 3 August 1546. Holland became the home of literature that was

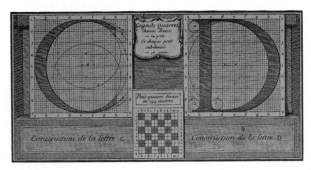

Construction de la lettre C   *Construction de la lettre D*

banned elsewhere. Lodewijk Elzevir made timely use of the situation to expand into the publication of small, pocket-sized books such as had been produced by Aldus Manutius in Venice.

Under the reign of Louis XIV, as the poor and the mad are confined, so letters are locked into the prison of the grid

The Abbé Jaugeon, of the French Académie des Sciences, was commissioned by the royal printers to design a new alphabet. Since this was the era of confinement, the letter was put behind bars and locked into diagrams of mathematical precision. Each letter was formed inside a square, which was itself composed of a grid divided into sixty-four smaller squares, constituting the archetype of typographical perfection.

It was Philippe Grandjean (1665–1714), an engraver whose temperament was rather that of an artist than a mathematician, who created the definitive form of the letter. Priding himself more on his good taste than on his geometry, in 1700 he designed the 'Romain du roi'. This typeface is today preserved at the Imprimerie Nationale in Paris.

In 1692 the Abbé Jaugeon, along with Filleau des Billettes and Sébastien Truchet, was given the task of 'describing the art of printing'. He endeavoured to find both the most visually attractive French types and a geometric system for drawing them, which would allow the greatest accuracy in reproduction. This grid is reminiscent of the grids used by the photocompositors of our own day.

During the first few decades of the history of printing, printers strove to imitate handwriting as closely as possible, for the convenience of the readers, who were used to manuscript books. The early large-format books were extremely expensive. The Italian printer Aldus was the first to think of producing small-format works, which were easier to handle and more reasonably priced. Right: Detail from a 17th-century French still life.

With the Enlightenment the world takes on a new aspect, and the eye requires something fresh and clear

Diderot's and D'Alembert's *Encyclopédie* had no use for embellishments or frills. It did not aim to embroider or

to decorate, but to clarify. By the 18th century interest in books had evolved considerably; the reader now sought information rather than mere visual pleasure. And in order to absorb information more readily, he had to be able to read with ease. With this in mind the Didots created a type that was representative of the new spirit.

The clarity and simplicity of the alphabet designed in 1755 by François-Ambroise Didot, and engraved by Pierre-Louis Wafflard, is exemplary. An exquisite construction of up- and downstrokes make 'Didot' the jewel of French typography.

In England, in 1716, William Caslon had designed a fine Roman typeface, which was to be used to print the American Declaration of Independence in 1776. John Baskerville acquired such a reputation that he had imitators as far away as France and Italy. One imitator

A style of 'E in O' in Grandjean type. After the engraver had cut the letters with the tip of a steel style, the founder would cast a matrix of copper, reproducing the letter in intaglio. Hundreds of characters could then be cast from this matrix using an alloy of lead and antimony.

This plate from the Diderot and D'Alembert *Encyclopédie* (opposite, left) shows the type (fig. 4), including the capital S and the various finer or wider spaces – known as leading – inserted by the typographer when he mounted a line in the galley (fig. 5). These would then be added to those already fixed in the printing forme (fig. 6).

of genius was an Italian, Giambattista Bodoni, who designed the 'Bodoni' font, inspired by the 'Garamonds' bought by Pope Sixtus V. 'Bodoni' spread throughout Europe and was used in England for newspaper type until the mid-20th century.

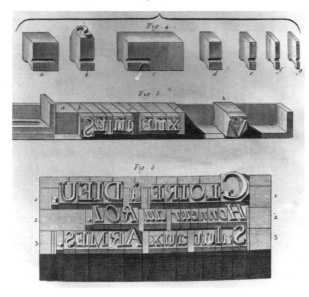

The type for the Didot capital E (above). A true dynasty, for two centuries the Didots maintained their reputation through an impressive number of refinements and inventions: the creation of vellum paper without the criss-crossed wiremarks; the definition of point size as a unit of typographic measure; and the perfection of the first machine to produce spooled paper.

New inventions change the history of writing

Until 1783 the hand press, which had remained almost unchanged since Gutenberg's time, could produce a maximum of three hundred sheets per day. At this date Didot added an iron bed and a copper plate to his machine. This metal press, which was undoubtedly the first of its kind, made it possible to print large-format sheets. At the same time the process for manufacturing paper on a spool was perfected. Fitted with a system for exerting pressure in 1807, the printing machine was improved again in 1812 when the system of flat plate against flat plate was replaced with a cylinder and reciprocating bed carrying the type forme. The first press of this kind, perfected by F. König, was set up in

England. At about the same time, the invention of the automatic inking-roller and the abandonment of the ink-ball also had the effect of speeding up the printing process. The production rate of the hand press had been some 250 to 300 sheets per day. With König's invention this increased to about 1100 sheets per hour, and the first four-cylinder press, invented by Augustus Applegath and Edward Cowper for *The Times* in 1828, enabled a production rate of some 4000 sheets per hour. Applegath and Cowper also invented a type-revolving press, which printed 8000 sheets per hour. By 1939 *The Times*, a thirty-two page paper, could be printed at a rate of some 40,000 copies per hour.

Setting up type by hand (left) was a lengthy process. The great innovation at the end of the 19th century was the introduction of matrices which the linotypist stored at the top of the machine. Once set up, the matrix made it possible to cast an entire line of characters at once. It was no longer a pack of letters, but a block of lines that the typographer placed on the bed.

The emphasis on speed initiated by the rotary press is confirmed towards the end of the 19th century by the invention of the Linotype

Since the time of Gutenberg compositors had had to assemble the texts letter by letter. Up to 1872 they picked out the letters and arranged them in lines, which they then placed in galleys and fitted onto a bed before fixing them in position using string and wooden pegs. Once the text had been printed they had to return the letters individually to their cases.

A skilled hand compositor was capable of composing a maximum of about fifteen hundred letters per hour. With the introduction of the Linotype, it became possible to work at a rate of up to nine thousand letters per hour. The change was considerable. Only the development of photocomposition in the 1930s was to prove of equal significance. Even then, the printing industry was not able to incorporate this system, and it was not until after World War Two that its advantages became fully apparent. To cover an event as it happened was no longer a dream. One historian writes: 'Five centuries later Gutenberg... would have been surprised, to say the least, to discover that newspapers, magazines and other printed matter had reduced books to

Marinoni's printing machine (below) came into service in France for the newspaper *La Presse* in 1847. Having been printed on the recto, each sheet would be turned automatically, reappearing with the verso presented ready for printing. *La Presse* was composed on four machines producing sixty thousand papers per hour, which, once trimmed and folded, were ready for distribution.

109

Printing images

The reproduction of pictures had begun in the Middle Ages with woodcuts, where the image stood out in relief like a block of type, and so could be combined with text. With the introduction of metal plates in the Renaissance, a finer image was made possible, incised into the metal by the engraver's burin or the etcher's acid (intaglio, or engraving, the opposite of relief) and printed on a special rolling press, which was necessary to exert greater pressure on the plate and paper. This is the process shown here. Engravings could not be combined with letterpress, however. To overcome this drawback a more refined version of the woodcut was invented, known confusingly as 'wood-engraving', using the fine end-grain of a hard wood. It was by this process that the great illustrated periodicals of the mid- and late 19th century were printed.

At the same time as printing machines were being developed, craft printing also survived. On the left the compositor and his case, which displays the lines of characters. In the centre two workers at the press: one attaches a sheet of paper to a frame which he is going to lower onto the printing forme; his colleague is inking the forme with a roller, a considerable step forward from the leather stamps covered with felt that had been used in Gutenberg's time. On the right are the type-casters; the lead is melted, then the characters are cast in sand matrices before being finished with a cold chisel.

representing only a modest proportion of published material'.

Colour printing was also speeded up by the invention of a machine able to print both sides of a page using different plates and inks. The same result is achieved on a much larger scale using giant rotary presses with as many rollers and elements as colours required – four, five or even more.

The progress of printing boosts the expansion of newspapers in the 18th century

The first periodicals had appeared at the beginning of the 17th century in the Netherlands and in Germany. By 1759 Dr Samuel Johnson was bemoaning the fact that in England 'Journals are daily multiplied, without increase of knowledge. The tale of the morning paper is told again in the evening, and the narratives of the evening are bought again in the morning.' It was, however, the French Revolution that introduced the concept of the freedom of the press, embodied in the Declaration of the Rights of Man in August 1789. More than three hundred newspapers appeared in France in the following year. They all

The 19th century saw a rapid growth in the newspaper press and its readership.
Above: A newspaper vendor cries his wares.

dreamed of imitating the pride of the English daily press, founded by John Walter in 1785 under the name of the *Daily Universal Register* and renamed *The Times* in 1788. The true forerunner of the great 'dailies' of contemporary opinion, this London daily acquired the nickname of *The Thunderer*, so outspoken were its editors in what they published. In 1815 it produced five thousand copies and in 1854, fifty thousand.

The lithographic process is perfected in the 18th century by a German living in Prague

Printing had reached a point where there was only one step missing: a process whereby the text and its illustrations could both be printed at the same time, using the same machine and the same paper.

In 1796 Aloïs Senefelder noticed that the limestone from the area around Solenhofen (near Munich) had the distinctive property that it rejected oil inks when they had been warmed. As a result of this observation, between 1796 and 1799 he invented a printing system based on the antipathy of oil and water, for which he obtained an English patent in 1800. This process was later expanded with the substitution of thin metal plates for the stone, and the use of photography (in 1840). Its most significant influence was on the rise of the poster after 1860.

The contemporary press failed to introduce any rapid modifications to the style or application of typography. In time, however, designers recognized the need to organize the way illustrations were used. And so the newspaper page became a changing format, favouring dialogue with the public, constituting one of the most powerful elements of modern publishing.

Even if books and newspapers are the domain of printing, some areas are still reserved for the pen

Correspondence, solicitors' documents and creative writing continued to be produced by hand well into the

One of the main reasons for the success of papers like *La Lune* (above) was the fact that they were so cheap. In England, once stamp duty on newspapers had been abolished in 1861, a daily paper cost only ½ *d* a copy – and so the popular press was born. The newspaper had become a consumer product.

"The first position is called 'face on', since the pen is held almost in line with the body, and in such a way as to produce thick down-strokes and diagonals. The second position is to the side; the pen is held so that the nib moves along the same plane as the horizontal line, producing thick strokes along this same line, as well as above and below the curves.... The third position is called 'inverse', since, because of the way it is held, the pen produces thick upward strokes."

Paillasson
The Art of Writing, 1763

20th century, and to a certain extent legal documents still require handwriting today, in that a personal signature is the only appropriate means of authenticating contracts, wills and sale documents. However, as the last domain of the public scribe, such legal documents helped to discredit the scribal profession, by associating it, in the eyes of the public, with the hated moneylenders who employed them. Despite their long and distinguished past, the status of these last professional calligraphers sank so low that by the end of the 19th century they were frequently dismissed as common drunkards.

In 1750, at Aachen, a magistrate named Johann Jantssen claimed to have invented a metal pen: 'Without

The early 19th-century engraving opposite, above, offers an unsympathetic image of the professional scribe.

wanting to boast, I believe that I can claim the honour of having invented a new pen'. The *Boston Mechanic,* on the other hand, claimed an American origin for the steel nib, saying that it had been invented by 'a well-known and honoured citizen of our town, Mr Peregrine Williamson'. According to a German publication of 1808, this invention can also be attributed to a schoolmaster near Königsberg, while a French pamphlet written in 1750 attributes the steel-nibbed pen to a Frenchman. In fact, it seems probable that it was perfected simultaneously in all these countries in response to general demand.

The greatest difficulty lay in reproducing the qualities of the goose-quill pen, and to begin with it seemed that only gold would provide the same suppleness. Hand-made steel nibs were so hard that they tore the paper. However, mechanical processes rapidly made it possible to produce high quality nibs in large numbers. Prices fell dramatically, and the steel nib thus became one of the first disposable products of our modern industrial civilization.

> **As Blaise Pascal said, 'To know how to write well is to know how to think well'**

From the 19th century onwards writing instruments improved and became more sophisticated. The need for greater accuracy and speed led to inventions such as the fountain pen, the ballpoint pen and the typewriter. The development of such tools has made the immense task of spreading literacy around the world ever easier, although it remains as yet uncompleted.

In December 1806 the poet William Wordsworth sent what he described as 'the longest letter I ever wrote in my life' to Lady Beaumont, wife of his friend Sir George Beaumont. He began by stating that 'notwithstanding I have the advantage of writing with one of your little pens' (referring to the then new, steel-nibbed variety, left), he would not be able to keep up the same standard of penmanship throughout.

Without the relentless perseverance of a few men, hieroglyphs, cuneiform and the Cretan Linear scripts would never have relinquished their secrets. Decipherers of the indecipherable, hunters in quest of hidden treasures, the men who uncovered the *terra incognita* of these written languages succeeded in bringing to light vast areas of our ancient history.

CHAPTER 6

THE DECIPHERERS

"Let us ask ourselves, positively, flatly, whether perhaps we should not admire those who deciphered hieroglyphs, cunciform or Cretan Linear B, a little more – or even much more – than those who designed the first pictograms, or who created a system for representing a complete vocabulary with a few alphabetic signs."
René Etiemble

It is not known who invented the infinite variety of modern scripts that have been used – and are still in use – throughout the world; nor will it ever be known. They come from an anonymous crowd of accountants, scribes and writing teachers. From the dawn of modern history such people have gradually worked to create the writing techniques that we use today.

However, those men who made it their mission to interpret the obscure signs that could be seen engraved on stone or inscribed in clay are people who are close to us in time, virtually contemporaries of ours. The first, and surely the most inspired of all, was Jean-François Champollion, who died in 1832. The decipherment of cuneiform began in the same era. As Béatrice Andrée Leicknam writes: 'The name of Sumer had remained unheard for over two thousand years. People were only just beginning to suspect that the ruins were going to produce the oldest writing system known to us.' As for Cretan script, Linear B, it was only finally deciphered around 1950–2 by Michael Ventris, who died in 1956.

The Rosetta Stone, 1.14 m high and 0.73 m wide, has always aroused the liveliest emotions amongst researchers. As early as August 1799 *Le Courrier d'Egypte* recorded that: 'This stone offers considerable scope for the study of hieroglyphs and may even give us the key to their decipherment.'

Though Champollion died at the age of forty-two, his short life was remarkably full and intense

From 1804, when he was a student at the Imperial Lycée in Grenoble, Champollion had been interested in

hieroglyphs. He studied Latin, Greek, Hebrew, Arabic, Syriac, Persian, Sanskrit, Chinese and Coptic, and soon became convinced that Coptic was simply a late form of the language that had been spoken in ancient Egypt.

In 1822, in a famous letter to André Dacier, permanent secretary to the Académie des Belles-Lettres in Paris, he expounded his theory 'concerning the phonetic alphabet used by the Egyptians to inscribe the titles, names and surnames of the ruling Greeks and Romans'. He was soon to prove this theory by applying it to the decipherment of the Rosetta Stone.

In 1824 he published *Le Précis du système hiéroglyphique des anciens Egyptiens (Description of the Hieroglyphic System of the Ancient Egyptians)*, and in 1828 he undertook a journey to Egypt, in the company of the artist Nestor L'Hôte, the stages of which he recorded in a feverishly enthusiastic diary. He died of exhaustion on his return to France.

Portrait of J.-F. Champollion in 1831.

The stela known as the Rosetta Stone had been discovered during Napoleon Bonaparte's expedition to Egypt in 1799. It was found near Rashid, a port located on the west branch of the Nile and to the east of Alexandria. It dates to 196 BC, when the priests, who had gathered at Memphis to celebrate the arrival of the twelve-year-old Ptolemy V, composed a decree in Greek in his honour. Copies of this decree were engraved on

In 1828 Nestor L'Hôte accompanied Champollion on his voyage to Egypt. His watercolours were annotated with observations such as this: 'The temple [of Maharaqa] is built in granite; it was never finished, and the only relief carvings are the hieroglyphs on the facade, which has fallen as one piece, and whose stones are still ranged in parallel on the ground'.

stone, preceded by translations in demotic and hieroglyphs.

The Rosetta Stone was seized by the English when they took Alexandria in 1801 during the long years of Franco-English rivalry for the domination of Egypt.

It was taken to the British Museum in London, where it can still be seen today. Champollion saw a copy of it in Paris in 1808, and studied it for several years. He established that the hieroglyphic text contained two cartouches. It was known that cartouches were used to surround royal names, two of which appeared in the Greek text: those of Cleopatra and of Ptolemy. For a long time it had been thought that all hieroglyphic signs were ideograms. Champollion's dazzling intuition led him to the idea that each sign represented not an entity, but a sound. His excellent command of Coptic and Greek enabled him to work out the meaning of the contents of the cartouches.

To read the Rosetta Stone it is necessary to follow the lion's gaze

He recognized that within the cartouches the text should be read from right to left and from top to bottom. Although such texts are usually read from left to right, the lion's gaze indicated the correct direction for reading this particular inscription.

Champollion recognized the name of Cleopatra from another stone, because the cartouche that contained it was on the upper part of the Rosetta Stone, which was partially destroyed. From this he was able to decipher the remaining text and to establish with certainty that

The Abbé Barthélemy was the first to put forward the theory that the oval frame (left) enclosed a royal name. From a Greek text citing Ptolemy V, Champollion attributed phonetic values to the hieroglyphs within the cartouche and read PTOLMYS.

A page from Champollion's manuscript of his great work on the decipherment of hieroglyphs (right), published in 1836. Here he is concerned with the way colours are used – sky is blue, earth red, the moon yellow etc. Men's clothes are always white; women's may be coloured. Women's skin is shown as yellow, men's as red.

14. Dans le premier Système applicable seulement aux Caractères Sculptés
en grand, on cherchait, par des teintes plattes, à rappeler
à peu près, la couleur naturelle des objets représentés : Ainsi les
Caractères figurants le Ciel. (1) était peints en bleu , la terre (2)
en Rouge ; la Lune (3) en Jaune , le Soleil (4) en Rouge , l'Eau en
bleu ou en verd (6)

1. ▬▬ 3. 🪐 5. ∿∿∿
2. ▬ 4. ● 6. ∿∿∿

15. Les Figures d'Hommes en pied sont peintes, sur les grands monuments
d'après des règles assez Constantes : les chairs sont en Rouge plus
ou moins foncé, les coiffures principalement en bleu et la tunique blanche,
les plis des draperies étant indiqués par des traits rouges

16. On donnait ordinairement des chairs jaunes aux figures de Femmes
et leurs Vêtements variaient en blanc, en verd ou en Rouge.

Les mêmes règles sont suivis dans le coloriage des hiéroglyphes écrites
en petit sur les Stèles et les Sarcophages : mais les vêtements sont tous
de couleur Verte.

hieroglyphs were not simply pictures, but that they represented sounds.

Champollion is exceptional for the way that he succeeded, almost unaided, in penetrating one of the most obscure mysteries of writing and in paving the way for the science of Egyptology.

The events in the long quest for the decipherment of cuneiform read like a thriller

The decipherment of cuneiform is the story of a team of scholars who, between 1800 and 1830, made momentous discoveries in the script of the ancient Near East.

It all began with a paper by Professor Georg Friedrich Grotefend (1775–1853) of Göttingen, who thought that he 'had deciphered the cuneiform inscriptions from Persepolis'. Rasmus C. N. Rask, Eugène Burnouf, Christian Lassen and especially Henry Creswicke Rawlinson (1810–95) carried these investigations further.

On a rock face at Behistun, in Persia, Rawlinson encountered a challenge similar to the one Champollion had faced with the Rosetta Stone: 'Of three columns of trilingual Persepolitan inscriptions, the first could be perfectly understood, and it must therefore be possible to work out the other two.' Edwin Norris discovered that the second language was Elamite. Other scholars, including Rawlinson, tried to interpret the third, and in 1851 met with success in translating the 112 lines of the third column. It was in Semitic Akkadian.

In 1857 the Royal Asiatic Society in London sent the same recently discovered inscription to four Assyriologists: Rawlinson, Edward Hincks, William H. Fox Talbot and Julius Oppert. They were to study it without consulting each other. One month later they

Orientalist, major-general, Member of Parliament, president of the Royal Asiatic Society and the Royal Geographical Society, in 1826 Henry Creswicke Rawlinson was an information officer in the Indian army, where he learnt Hindustani, Arabic and modern Persian. During a diplomatic tour of duty in Persia in 1833, he undertook the decipherment of cuneiform, becoming the 'Champollion' of the rock at Behistun (below right; a detail is shown left). He made drawings on the site at the risk of his life.

all returned their translations, which proved in all essentials to be the same.

In 1905 François Thureau-Dangin (1872–1944) produced the first translation of Sumerian, man's earliest identified writing.

And since the beginning of the 20th century progress in the area of decipherment has continued unabated. As Jean Bottéro writes: 'In the whole history of History there can have been no greater experience than that which, in less than a century, has led scholars from the first spark, which no one paid much attention to, to a blaze of discovery and understanding... and which has brought to light vast and significant areas of our past that seemed until then to be forever lost in time!'

Nevertheless, there are certain puzzles that still remain to be solved.

"The upper inscriptions can only be copied by standing on the topmost step of the ladder, with no other support than steadying the body against the rock with the left arm, while the left hand holds the notebook and the right hand is employed with the pencil. In this position I copied all the upper inscriptions, and the interest of the occupation entirely did away with any sense of danger"

Henry C. Rawlinson

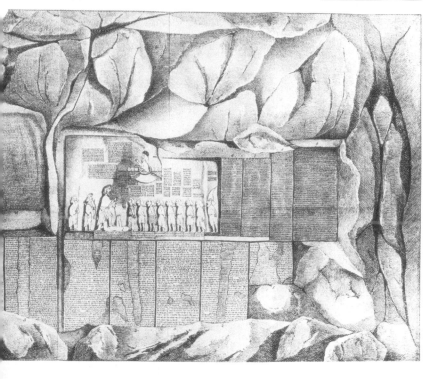

In Crete three scripts continue to mystify the experts

In 1900 the English archaeologist Sir Arthur John Evans discovered some fragments of clay tablets in the ruins of the ancient palace at Knossos in Crete; they bore inscriptions that appeared to be some form of writing.

The oldest, which was very fragmentary, was dated to between 2000 and 1650 BC. The second, which Evans called Linear A, was later dated to between 1750 and 1450 BC. To this day no one has succeeded in deciphering this script properly. Finally, Evans established the fact that a third script, the date of which was uncertain, and which he named Linear B, had replaced Linear A. There was a large number of tablets with this Linear writing, and Evans put forward many theories and suggestions for the decipherment of the script before his death in 1941.

A reconstruction of the palace at Knossos, in Crete, excavated by Sir Arthur Evans. According to him, the town alone, situated 4 km from the sea and including the palace and principal houses, had some 80,000 inhabitants. Together with the port, the present-day town of Heraklion, the population of Knossos could have reached 100,000 inhabitants.

Five years before Evans' death a schoolboy vows to continue his work

In 1936 Evans had held a conference in London on the theme of 'this long forgotten civilization of ancient Crete and the mysterious writing system used by its people'.

In the audience was a fourteen-year-old boy who was passionately interested in ancient languages. The teenager's name was Michael Ventris, and on that day at Burlington House he vowed that he would be the one to solve the puzzle of the apparently indecipherable Cretan script.

He began writing to scholars and eventually succeeded where those before him had failed. Michael Ventris' achievement was not only to decipher Linear B, but also to demonstrate beyond any doubt that it was the writing system used by the Mycenean inhabitants of continental Greece at the time when those who were to become the legendary heroes of Homer were living there. He achieved this as the result of a succession of tiny, apparently contradictory discoveries.

John Chadwick, his friend and colleague, summed up the nature of Ventris' particular genius – a genius that characterizes all decipherers: 'Ventris was able to see, in the confusing diversity of these signs, an overall pattern and to pinpoint certain constants which revealed the underlying structure. It was this quality – the gift of being able to make order out of apparent confusion – that is the sign of greatness amongst the scholars in this field.'

Linear signs (here Linear B is shown), used during the Minoan periods, appear on clay tablets, and on objects found not only on the island but throughout the Cycladic Islands, and even into Greece itself. Hence the generally held theory that Cretan derives from Achaean, a language spoken by the Greeks in the 2nd millennium BC. Certain ideograms are easily identifiable, but the interpretation of others remains obscure, as does the language that hides behind this writing.

From Phaistos to Easter Island, there are still many undeciphered signs

Since the death of Ventris there has been continuing research, but without tangible results. Neither Linear A nor the Phaistos disc, for example, has as yet given up its secrets. Equally, certain aspects of the Maya writing

system and the strange signs that cover the wooden writing boards of Easter Island, from the language known as Rongo-Rongo, continue to preserve their mystery. However, with patience, enthusiasm and lucidity, men have succeeded in deciphering almost all writing systems, including such oddities as Scandinavian runes and Ogham, the oldest Celtic writing system known, from Wales and Ireland.

The areas of writing that remain obscure constitute possibly the most absorbing aspect of the subject, as much because of our fascination with the genius of those who invented the scripts as with that of those who deciphered them. Some people remain dazzled by the beauty of the signs, which seem to speak for themselves without the need for translation. A narrative full of enigmas, the story of writing is the story of a complex metamorphosis. Begun six thousand years ago to serve for the keeping of records, writing became a way of thinking, of conceiving ideas, of creating and of being. It remains, in the words of Roland Barthes, 'a necessary part of any fully functioning language'.

Discovered in 1721 by the Dutchman Jacob Roggeveen, the Moas, monumental statues set into the earth on Easter Island, seem to symbolize a secret of eternity. And to this day, the wooden tablets and the stones, with over five hundred different signs carved by the same hands that erected the statues, remain unintelligible.

DOCUMENTS

On the borderline between art and
technology stands writing.
Throughout history humanity has
used it to record the boundless
variety of writing itself: typography
and calligraphy to please the eye,
signs and symbols to satisfy the
mind, games to amuse and
graffiti to provoke.

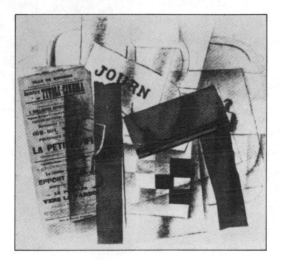

The letter and the city

In the modern world, and in particular under the influence of advertising, the letter has become a separate entity. Removed from the mass of words, sundered from all semantic associations, it has become a visual experience, whether it be an institutionalized one, as in advertising, or a freer form, such as graffiti. Today, the letter has become a landmark in the everyday world.

In our Western civilization, the letter is evolving from an abstract representation back into a visual image. Below is a dizzying catalogue of the letter-pictures that are invading our everyday lives.

Broadway, that great artery of New York, and its epicentre, Times Square, have the highest typographical density in the world.

The neon cinema boards, temples of light, in 42nd Street. The gigantic Hotel Stardust neon board in Las Vegas that uses fifteen thousand lightbulbs; that of Macy's in New York, 'The World's Largest Store', which covers six storeys. The average American may see up to fifteen hundred advertising signs in any one day. The highest concentration of these visual images is achieved in Las Vegas and in Hong Kong (during the day as well as at night), where the street is a continual display of shapes and colours.

The city is like an enormous open book, written by an anonymous hand. It is enough just to look; the images speak for themselves.

Service stations bristling with masts, poles and banners whose giant headlines ring out in the sunshine.

Advertisements in the underground suspended above sleeping passengers.

Walls talking to you through speech bubbles, balloons carrying words high in the air, or whirling aeroplanes writing messages across the sky.

Pillar-shaped billboards with torn posters making unrecognizable slogans. Graffiti.

Forgotten signs from the last century.

Chalked up prices on market stall noticeboards, packing crates covered with exotic lettering, fairground extravaganzas.

The grocer's shop with its window a checkerboard of multicoloured posters;

the wall of paper offered in newspaper kiosks; the colourful puzzles made by Parisian drugstore windows; cafe windows praising their wares in Gothic lettering (banana split, ice cream soda); white chalk scribblings; the awnings outside shops, the competitive sales signs, the announcements of closing down sales that cover whole facades in banners.

Giant price tickets from bargain basements, painted walls, gaily-coloured houses, hippies' messages – 'We love you', Italian obituary notices, registration numbers, street plans.

Newspapers, magazines, prospectuses, tracts, posters, directions, post, telegrams, books, dictionaries, phone books, theses, directions for use, geographical maps, classified advertisements and love letters. Teleprinter printouts, cartoon strips, tokens, tickets and banknotes, hand-written menus, booksellers' windows and those of estate agents. And all the moving neon lights, the flickering words, letters climbing up the signs or tumbling down. Vehicles carrying advertisements, sandwich-men and garish carrier bags all adding to the mêlée among the pedestrians.

The mysterious arithmetic that covers freight cars, and the flow of figures on a calculator.

The Cuba pavilion in Montreal – subversive, dramatic, completely typographical, walls, floor and ceiling.

Signposts with their many arms, all the placards overhanging the road, looming out from the house fronts and gables, or appearing from recesses, streaking empty spaces with colour and climbing to attack the upper floors.

The little signs, 'Don't feel awkward any more – learn to dance', which hang from the Parisian guttering, slot machines, pinball machines, letter boxes, tattered posters shivering in the wind,

lettering on the road surface, council notices, campaign posters, sales booths for tickets in the French *Loterie Nationale*, timetables, street signs, signs saying 'Bill stickers will be prosecuted', or 'Please show proof of identity'.

And all those warnings of 'Danger', 'Fragile', 'Wet paint', 'Emergency exit', 'Police', 'Wait', 'No parking (Sunday parade)', 'No entry', not to mention all those eye- and hand-level commands: 'In', 'Out', 'Up', 'Down', 'Pull', 'Push'.

Robert Massin
Letter and Image, 1972

The implications of writing

The general implications of introducing a means of recording speech are revolutionary. How did it change the world of man? What did writing facilitate?

The invention of the alphabet, and to some extent that of the syllabary, led to an enormous reduction in the number of signs, and to a writing system which was potentially unrestricted both in its capacity to transcribe speech and in its availability to the general population. The descendants of the Canaanite alphabet spread widely through Europe and Asia, and later the remaining continents, making available a script that was easy to learn and easy to use.

The results are seen in the apparent growth of literacy in the Syrian–Palestinian area, where the uses of writing expanded from the political and economic to the religious and the historical-literary: of this the Old Testament of the Hebrews may be

Isis inscription in the church of St John the Divine on Ios showing Greek writing of the 2nd or 3rd century AD.

The charter of Julius Caesar's colony at Urso (Osuna), inscribed in Latin on bronze tablets.

Part of one of the Dead Sea Scrolls, containing the Book of Isaiah, written in Hebrew script of the 1st century BC.

considered one of the first great products. However, the real extension of literacy, certainly as far as the range of writing was concerned, took place in Greece, with its fully developed alphabet and a system of instruction that placed literacy outside the constraint of a religious system. In this new context, writing managed to place some restrictions on the development of centralized government, which it helped to promote, by providing an instrument of control in the shape of the ballot. At the same time, it saw the development of new fields of knowledge as well as encouraging new ways of knowing; the development of the visual scrutiny of text now supplemented the aural input of sound over wide areas of human understanding; linguistic information was organized by means of tangible records, which affected the way in which man's practical intelligence, his cognitive processes, could work on the world around. This potential was there with logo-syllabic systems; indeed, in China great advances in the accumulation and development of knowledge have been made using the earliest system of full writing. But the development of a democratic form of writing, one that could make the easy transcription of language a possibility for the vast majority of the community, followed the invention of the alphabet in the Near East, though it was not until the invention of mechanical reproduction of these texts by means of movable type that the alphabet came into its own.

Jack Goody
Contact, Human Communication and its History, 1981

The typographer's art

As soon as type had been invented, there was a potential conflict between form and content. The form is the printed book. The content is the subject-matter conveyed through the book. For two centuries the contribution of typographers was negligible. Then the conflict resolved itself. From the 19th century onwards the dynamics of the art of typography united the signifier and the signified.

Tory, pupil of Dürer and Leonardo

Tory enclosed in the O (a perfect circle) the seven liberal arts, and entrusted to the care of the I – the other fundamental letter – the task of representing the nine muses. Then, encouraged no doubt by the boldness of his work, and undaunted by the challenge of any acrobatic form, he brought together the seven liberal arts and the nine muses under the aspect of a flageolet (a type of flute with seven stops), which, seen end-on and in foreshortening, is at once an upright O and a prone I.

These two letters allow the meeting of the straight line and the circle, and they therefore symbolize the two organs of generation; from this union, placed under the sign of the goddess Io, are born all the letters of the alphabet....

Lastly, with the help of the eye and a pair of compasses, Tory positioned all the letters that constituted the alphabet of his time around a central O, representing a sun whose twenty-three rays correspond to the nine muses, the seven liberal arts, the four cardinal virtues and the three graces.

Of the twenty-three letters reviewed in the *Champ-Fleury* [of 1529], described, annotated, and detailed with meticulous care,... some deserve closer scrutiny.

The letter A 'has its legs apart in the manner of a man's legs and feet as he strides along'. Moreover, the cross-bar of the A 'precisely covers the man's genital organ, to denote that modesty and chastity above all else are required in those who seek access and admission to good letter forms, among which A is the entrance gate and first in order in all ABCs.'

Elsewhere Tory constructs the A from a ruler and a pair of compasses, which represent respectively the queen and king.

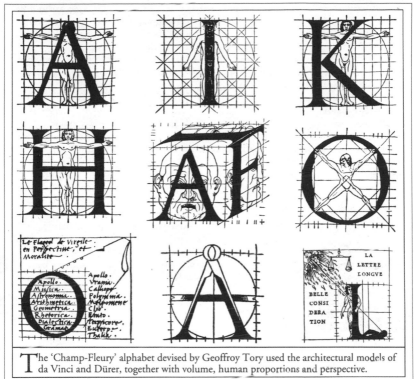

The 'Champ-Fleury' alphabet devised by Geoffroy Tory used the architectural models of da Vinci and Dürer, together with volume, human proportions and perspective.

The letter D is in the image of 'a theatre stage, like the one I saw in a city near Avignon'.... This stage, which 'is straight at the front and circular at the back, can well be taken as the letter D'.

The letter H represents 'the body of a house, read so that the part below the horizontal line – which I have stipulated as being centrally placed and extending across the diameter – represents the lower halls and chambers. The part above it similarly represents the great halls or great and middling chambers'.

The letter I: 'I cannot pass on here without pointing out that our said letters were devised through divine inspiration.

Homer, king of the Greek poets, states at the beginning of Book VIII of his *Iliad* that Jupiter once said he could, if he so wished, draw to himself by means of a golden chain all the other gods, and even the earth and the sea as well.' If we imagine this golden chain hanging down from the heavens to our feet, we see that it is 'well proportioned in length and breadth, suited to the symmetry of our proportional letter I'.

The theme of this golden chain runs through Tory's work, sometimes associated with other allegorical images, such as that of the Golden Bough, 'which has twenty-three leaves as a hidden sign of the twenty-three letters of the alphabet'. This last image, borrowed from Virgil, shows the antique and Italian influences on Tory. 'I have seen the Colosseum more than a thousand times', he said. When it was intact, the Colosseum was shaped like the letter O, 'circular outside and oval within'.

The letter L makes reference to another allegory under the sign of Libra. It derives its form from the image of a human body and its shadow, as cast when 'the sun is in the sign of the Balance'. The letter M, for its part, is

Letter V by Honoré Daumier, 1836.

the object of a far more prosaic interpretation: 'it is like some men, who are so stout that their belt is longer than their body is tall'.

But it is certainly the letter Q that gives rise to the most amusing image. Having noticed that 'this said letter Q is the only one amongst all the letters which extends below the line', he found nobody who could provide him with a satisfactory explanation for this. Tory continues: 'I have pondered so much, and ruminated on these so-called Attic letters, and have concluded that the letter Q has a tail because it will not allow itself to be written in proper usage without its companion and good brother U: to show that he always wants him to follow, he embraces him with his tail.'

To pronounce the letter S is to 'make a whistling sound as strident as a hot iron when it is plunged in water'.

Finally, the letter Y, like the 'vanities' depicted by Tory's contemporaries, is the emblem of pleasures and virtues.

Geoffrey Tory foresaw that he was bound to attract criticism. 'I don't doubt that detractors and bores will yap', he prophesied, but that would not prevent him from writing about his 'fantasy and speculation, to give pleasure and service to good students'.

An enemy of all things pedantic, Tory was one with Rabelais (who was possibly born in the same year) in lightness of spirit, even in his humorous way with words. Here, by way of a sample, is the opening of the first book of the *Champ-Fleury*:

'On the morning of Epiphany, having had my fill of sleep and rest, and my stomach having effortlessly digested its light and joyful meal, in the year 1523, I took to imagining in my bed, turning the wheel of memory, thinking of a thousand little fantasies – solemn as well as joyful – amongst which came back to me the memories of a certain antique letter that I had once designed.'

Robert Massin
Letter and Image, 1972

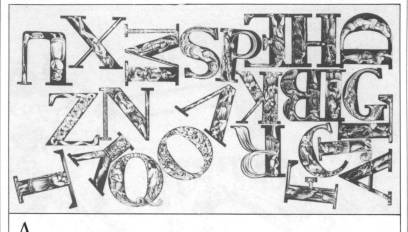

An alphabet made up of human figures, 1836.

The work of the typographer, like that of all other artisans, is closely linked to the era in which he lives, and is governed by the requirements and methods of his time. There are two aspects to his job: on the one hand he must produce the required end result, and on the other he must express himself as an artist.

The formal and the useful: two qualities that have always been determined by contemporary fashion, which has alternatively stressed form or function. Occasionally there have been special periods when form and function have achieved an element of balance and unity.

The specialist literature of recent years has consistently called for a typographical style suited to modern times. In 1931 Paul Renner wrote: 'A printing works is not intended to hire out fancy dress. Its role is not to deck out a literary text in a fashionable disguise, but rather to make certain that it appears in a style appropriate to its era. It does not wish to be anything other than a living typographical work, and not a masquerade.'...

With the benefit of hindsight, every era can be seen as a distinct period with its own solidly defined image. Gothic characters show a striking relationship to other works of the same period; the Art Nouveau style of the early 20th century is reflected in the typography of Otto Eckmann, and the Constructivism of the Twenties in that of the Bauhaus. For people at the time each period never appears clear-cut; on the contrary, it seems to be chaotic and disconcerting.

However, we in the 20th century must try to isolate the significant characteristics of our age. These characteristics stem from our attempts to find viable solutions to contemporary problems, and it is in this area that printed works can bear accurate witness to some of the unrecognized features of our time. The various disciplines of art are not self-contained, and typography can only flourish by being part of the

Playful typography: *Words in Futurist Freedom*, 1919, by Filippo Marinetti.

general flux of events. Otherwise it would be condemned to sterility. But it has its own laws and restrictions imposed by its technical nature, which help it to preserve a certain independence and thus escape fruitless servitude.

If on occasion one regrets the facility with which typography absorbs the trends of the day, it must be recognized that this is infinitely preferable to a completely detached existence, which would be fatal.

Accepting all this, the true creative artist pays no heed to fashion; he knows that conscious effort does not come into the search for a particular style, and that this style will only result from a slow, subconscious process.

Technology, precision and order find better expression in typography than they do in graphic design. With typography it is not a matter of fulfilling lofty artistic demands, or of satisfying a creative instinct; it satisfies the more practical aspects of creativity, performing the formal and functional requirements of a craft. The mechanical production of the characters and the creation of a layout dictated by strictly defined measurements require both a rigorous framework and clearly ordered relationships.

Tabular works offer the typographer the best way of demonstrating his skill in arranging his material. Nevertheless, he must not allow purely formal considerations to take over. A technical charm, even a certain beauty, emanates from a well laid-out table, and the most mundane railway timetable can prove to be a more satisfyingly crafted piece of work than some chance design full of fancy shapes and colours.

But typography can also play a part in advertising. We need printed works that will catch the eye in our modern world, where ideas and products are constantly competing for attention. The art of typography lies in the ability to interpret and structure the text using characters carefully selected from the countless fonts available, ranging from wide to narrow and large to small. For his work the typographer selects fonts that harmonize well; in this context one need only look at the twenty variant forms of 'Univers', which provide a well-graded, carefully thought-out range.

Let us hope that typefaces of this kind will set an example of order and harmony in the more or less chaotic state of affairs that exists in typecasting today.

Many printed works are attractive purely because the typographer has put aside his artistic pretensions and simply allowed the print to do its own job. It was Stanley Morison's belief that a typographic composition should be a useful and precise piece of work, fit for its purpose as a means of communication.

The worlds of Baroque architecture and of Far Eastern art and philosophy all hold that a created form and its counter-form arising in space are of equal importance. Part of the reason why modernists now have a renewed interest in Baroque architecture is that it involves the integration of space into form, a characteristic of the Baroque period, which is now being explored in modern terms. Large cubes joined together form living space, and the empty space

between the buildings forms part of the overall scheme; it provides a free space, an area 'where people can congregate or stroll about, depending on the demands of business, conversation or just sweet leisure' (Jakob Burkhardt).

According to the philosophy of the Far East, it is only empty space that engenders the essence of the created form. Without the hollow inside, a jug is nothing more than a lump of clay; the only thing that makes it a container is its empty internal space. Hence the eleventh saying of Lao-Tse:

'Thirty spokes converge towards the hub, but it is the space between them that forms the essence of the wheel.

'From clay come jars, but it is the emptiness inside them that holds the nature of the jar.

'The walls, with the windows and doors attached to them, form the house, but it is the empty space within that creates the essence of the house.

'This is the rule. The material harbours usefulness and the immaterial imparts the true essence.'

These principles can and must be adopted in typography. Unlike during the Renaissance, when the blank areas of a printed page were held to be of secondary importance, modern typography has long recognized that unprinted space has a relevant value of its own in any design. The typographer employs blank spaces as a formal element, and also knows how to exploit the optical variations that occur within white areas....

Rhythm moves the whole world, and in this way rhythm is at the source of all life. Every creature grows and develops at rhythmic intervals, and the rhythmic blowing of the wind moves smoke, trees, fields of grain and sand dunes. The coming of machines has made us more

aware of the full value of a working rhythm, and it is recognized that the mental and physical well-being of workers depends heavily on a well-structured, rhythmical work routine.

Over the centuries works of art have transmitted all shades of rhythmic sensation. In the 20th century, especially, the deeper meaning and strength of rhythm in design have been expressed with great clarity.

**eingekeilt eingekeilt eingekeilt eing
keilt eingekeilt eingekeilt eingekeilt
eingekeilt eingekeilt eingekeilt eing
keilt eingekeilt eingekeilt eingekeilt
eingekeilt eingekeilt eingekeilt eing
keilt eingekeilt eingekeilt eingekeilt
eingekeilt eingekeilt eingekeilt eing
keilt eingekeilt eingekeilt eingekeilt
eingekeilt eingekeilt eingekeilt eing
keilt eingekeilt eingekeilt eingekeilt
eingekeilt eingekeilt eingekeilt eing
keilt eingekeilt eingekeilt eingekeilt
eingekeilt eingekeilt eingekeilt eing
keilt eingekeilt eingekeilt eingekeilt
eingekeilt eingekeilt eingekeilt eing
keilt eingekeilt eingekeilt eingekeilt
eingekeilt eingekeilt eingekeilt eing
keilt eingekeilt eingekeilt eingekeilt
eingekeilt eingekeilt eingekeilt eing**

There are countless ways in which the typographer can express rhythmic values. The printed characters of a typeface are all rhythmic images, whether they be composed of straight, curved, vertical, horizontal or oblique elements. A simple text is full of rhythmic values: ascenders and descenders, pointed or rounded forms, symmetrical or asymmetrical lines. Spacing gives a rhythmic structure to the lines and the composition as a whole, by creating words of greater or lesser length, just as a musical phrase is punctuated by variable tempos and heavier or lighter stresses. Ends of paragraphs and line spaces also structure the composition, and the graded sizes of the type give the typographic work that shape and general rhythm that characterize it. Even the simplest typography, providing it is well composed, will impart an appealing sense of rhythm.

The shape of the paper forms another rhythmic element; it might be the symmetry of an equilateral square or the stressed rhythm of the short and long edges of a rectangle. Endless possibilities are available to the typographer in the way he organizes his composition on the page. The rhythm of the composition can be in harmony with the format of the paper, or in contrast to it. When designing a composition, the typographer should endeavour to find every possible means of getting away from rigid formats and dull repetition – not just for the sake of bringing vitality to the form, but also in the interests of legibility.

Emil Ruder
Typography, 1981

Im Saal des
Restaurant Bären
Grellingen
Schmutziger Donnerstag
20 Uhr

MASKEN BALL

Bar und Weinstube
Eintritt 3.50
Maskierte 2.-
Es ladet ein.
das Orchester
Les diables rouges
der Wirt und
Jahrgang 45

GROSSER
MAS

Early printing in Europe

In less than thirty-five years, between 1454 and 1487, printing spread throughout Europe. The first printers strove to make their books look as much like hand-written manuscripts as possible, introducing elaborately decorated capitals, which were probably stamped in after the pages had been printed, and ligatures between the letters. The title page of the Slavonic Bible of 1663 is as richly ornamented as any illuminated manuscript of the Middle Ages.

Above right: A page of the 'Forty-two line' Bible, *c.* 1455, traditionally ascribed to Johannes Gutenberg. Below right: William Caxton's *The Doctrinal of Sapience,* printed at Westminster, *c.* 1489.

Opposite: Cyrillic printing – the title page of the Slavonic Bible, *Biblia Russica,* 1663, which was part of a campaign by Patriarch Nikon to remedy ignorance and superstition among the clergy.

From pen to print

Paradoxically, just at the moment when printing seemed ready to replace handwriting altogether, the art of writing took on new life. The 16th century saw the appearance in Italy of classic manuals on the subject, which have remained definitive ever since.

In the 1440s a type of writing known as 'Chancery' had been adopted at the papal court. Based on Carolingian letters, it soon became popular all over Europe because of its elegance and legibility, and it is the basis of what we today call 'italic', after its Italian origins.

a – *Tondo dela penna* .
b – *Canaletto* .
c – *Curuita* .
d – *Primo taglio* .
e' – *Secondi tagli* .
f – *Vomero* .
g – *Sguizo* .
h – *Punta temperata* .

In 1522 Chancery script appeared in printed form for the first time in Ludovico Arrighi's *La Operina da imparare di scrivere littera cancellarescha* ('How to write the Chancery hand'). The page shown opposite displays abbreviations for ceremonial superlatives used in elaborate, formal modes of address – 'Famosissima', 'Revendissima' etc. – arranged in alphabetical order. The illustration above shows how to prepare a quill pen as a writing instrument.

Amant.mo .A. Beat.mo Car.o . Car.mo . Char.mo

Dign.mo . E.mo . C.sa xij . R. Pn. Famos.mo

Gnoso. A.on Hon.mo . Hon . Ill.mo

Ill.mo . Ill. . Ill.mo . Ill.88o ill.mo . K.to

L. M.tias . Mag.tia Mag.co . Nobil.mo . O

Rincipi Pres.to R.mo Reueren

Scr.mo San.tias T.T Ven.us Vra X.mo

yX

.na Uicentin. Scibeba.

SONETTO.

D oue' son gli occhi, et la serena forma.
del santo allegro, et amoroso aspetto?
dou'e la man eburna ou e'l bel petto.
ch'appensarui hor'in fonte'mi transforma?

In 1530 Giovanniantonio Tagliente's *Lo presente libro insegna* (above left) was published. Tagliente could teach all kinds of writing, from Chancery to Gothic black letter (above right). He could even write Hebrew.

Finally, in 1540, came the *Libro Nuovo* of Giovanbattista Palatino. Palatino was a learned man who loved languages and linguistic games. He printed works in Chaldean, Arabian, Egyptian, Indian, Syriac, Cyrillic, and what he calls 'Saracen' alphabets. He also enjoyed rebus writing – a modern form of hieroglyphics – in which words are represented by objects whose names coincide with the sound required. For instance, in the example shown opposite,

dove ('where') is represented by a D, followed by a picture of two eggs, *uove*.

In England the most famous and popular of all writing manuals was George Bickham's 'The Universal Penman', published in 1741. His elaborate title page (shown overleaf) sets out his aims and purposes at length. The book contained a wealth of examples, not only of penmanship, but of moral precepts and counsels of prudence.

Writing is the first Step, and Essential in furnishing out the Man of Business. And this Qualification is more excellent, as 'tis more useful in Business, and beautiful to the Eye, & may not improperly be consider'd in two Respects, as it proceeds from the Eye and the Hand; From the one, we have Size and Proportion; From the other, Boldness and Freedom. For as the Exactness of the Eye fixes the Heights and Distances; so the Motion of the Joints, and Position of the Hand, determine the black and fine Strokes, and give the same Inclination and Likeness in the Standing Turn of the Letters.

But, in Order to write well, there must be just Rules given, and much Practice to put 'em in Execution. Plain, Strong, and neat Writing, as it best answers the Design for Use and Beauty; so it has most obtain'd among Men of Business. A full, free, open Letter, struck at once, as it discovers more of Nature, so it gives a Masterly Beauty to the Writing; to which may be added such ornamental Turns of the Pen, as seem rather design'd to fill up Vacancies on the Paper, than studiously compos'd to adorn the Piece. In Flourishing the Fancy would be so Luxuriant, was it not corrected by the Judgement, as almost to destroy the End of Writing; as Airs in Musick, when too often repeated, or too long or too variously performed, disorder the Harmony of a just Composure.

But, as above, if Usefulness and Beauty are the Excellencies of Writing; that which will, with the greatest Facility, contribute to these, is the best Method of Teaching. Supposing, therefore, the Make and Proportion of the Letters and Joinings to be once well fixed and understood, and then if the Learner is us'd to copy the great Variety of Examples which are here produc'd, his Hand will grow confirm'd in an Aptitude and Readiness, which will insensibly arrive at Perfection and Dispatch; and give in Writing what we admire in fine Gentlemen; an Easiness of Gesture, and disengag'd Air, which is imperceptibly caught from frequently conversing with the Polite and Well-bred.

George Bickham
The Universal Penman, 1741

On the art of writing

Hail mistick Art! which men like Angels taught,
To speak to Eyes, and paint unbody'd Thought!
Tho' Deaf, and Dumb; blest Skill, reliev'd by Thee
We make one Sense perform the Task of Three.
We see, we hear, we touch the Head and Heart;
And take, or give, what each but yield in part.
With the hard Laws of Distance we dispence,
And without Sound, apart, commune in Sense;
View, tho' confin'd; nay, rule this Earthly Ball,
And travel o'er the wide expanded All.
Dead Letters, thus with Living Notions fraught,
Prove to the Soul the Telescopes of Thought;
To Mortal Life a deathless Witness give;
And bid all Deeds and Titles last, and live.
In scanty Life, Eternity we taste;
View the First Ages, and inform the Last.
Arts, Hist'ry, Laws, we purchase with a Look,
And keep, like Fate, all Nature in a Book.

Joseph Champion
Early 18th century

The title page of George Bickham's *The Universal Penman* of 1741.

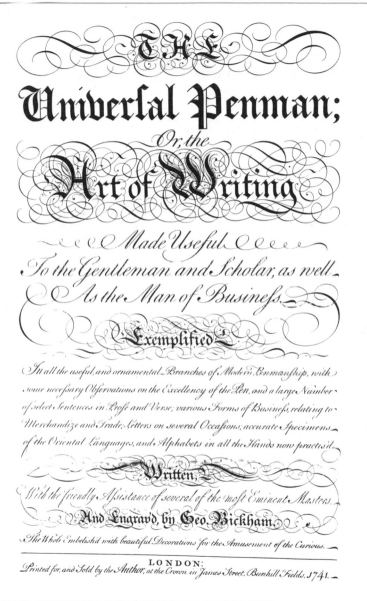

THE
Universal Penman;
Or, the
Art of Writing
Made Useful
To the Gentleman and Scholar, as well
As the Man of Business.

Exemplified

In all the useful, and ornamental Branches of Modern Penmanship, with some necessary Observations on the Excellency of the Pen, and a large Number of select Sentences in Prose and Verse; various Forms of Business, relating to Merchandize and Trade; Letters on several Occasions; accurate Specimens of the Oriental Languages, and Alphabets in all the Hands now practis'd.

Written,
With the friendly Assistance of several of the most Eminent Masters.
And Engrav'd, by Geo. Bickham.
The Whole Embelish'd with beautiful Decorations for the Amusement of the Curious.

LONDON:
Printed for, and Sold by the Author, at the Crown in James Street, Bunhill Fields, 1741.

Writing music

Writing is a witness, a seismograph of sentiment as well as of meaning. It records, it translates. Written music is, more than any other kind of writing, a form of notation. As well as the length of sounds, the distance between them, the tempo and shape of each phrase, musical notation translates the dynamics and the strength of emotion. When a musician reads a score, he hears it.

Notation for a trumpet solo by the American composer John Cage.

Problems of notation

As a musician, one is constantly confronted with the problem of how a composer arranges his ideas and his intentions, and how he attempts to transmit them both to his contemporaries and to posterity. One constantly witnesses the limitations imposed on these efforts, and the attempts made by various composers to avoid ambiguity in the less precise areas of transcription.

Each composer creates a personal style of notation, which today can only be deciphered by studying it within its particular historical context. It is still a common but serious error to assume that the notes, indications of character and movement, as well as the more subtle nuances of interpretation, have always had the same values that they possess today.

This assumption has been encouraged by the fact that over the centuries the same graphic signs have been used to transcribe music, without sufficient heed being paid to the fact that notation is not simply a timeless and international method of transcribing music, valid throughout the centuries; the meaning of different signs has changed in accordance with the changing styles of music and the composers and performers.

Some of these different meanings can be studied in books written specifically to instruct; in other cases they must be deduced from the musical and philological context. However, this is a method that always carries with it some risk of error.

Notation is thus like an extremely complex rebus system. Anyone who has ever tried to translate a musical idea or a rhythmic structure into notes knows that it is a relatively simple exercise. But when one asks a musician to play what is

G_{LO-} RI- A in ex-cel-sis De- o. Et in ter- râ pax ho- mi- ni-bus bo·næ

Gregorian chant from *Messes sur divers tons*, 18th century, based on the Roman gradual.

written, what he plays is not at all what one expects.

Our form of notation is intended to tell us both the individual notes and the shape of the piece of music. But any musician will tell you that this notation is very inexact, and that it does not say precisely what it means: it gives no indication of the length of a sound, nor of its pitch, nor any indication of tempo, since the technical criteria necessitated by these requirements cannot be transcribed using notation. The precise length of a note can only be indicated by means of a unit of time; the pitch of a note can only be accurately represented by a frequency; a constant tempo can be indicated by a metronome, but such a tempo does not exist.

Is it not astonishing that two pieces of music that are completely different in essence and style – for example a scene from an opera by [Claudio] Monteverdi and a symphony by Gustav Mahler –

Facsimile of a manuscript for a cello suite by Johann Sebastian Bach.

A portrait of Beethoven, calligraphed using a fragment from one of his sonatas, 1972.

have to be written using the same notation? When one becomes aware of the enormous differences between the diverse genres of music, it must seem strange that for music of every age and of every conceivable style only some fifteen hundred signs have been used.

Despite this similarity in the signs, it is possible to discern two radically different principles governing their usage: either it is the *work*, the composition itself, which is put into writing, with no detailed indication of how it is to be executed; or it is the *execution* of the work that is indicated, the notation being essentially an indication of what and how it should be played.

This second method does not show (as in the first case) the form and structure of the composition, which must be acquired from other sources, but only, as precisely as possible, the sounds that are to be reproduced: this, it says, is how it should be played – the work then 'materializes', so to speak, from the act of playing.

As a general rule it can be said that up until 1800 written music consisted of transcribing the *work*, and thereafter the *method of execution*. There are, however, numerous overlaps; for example, diagrams to show the positioning of the fingers for certain instruments from about the 16th and 17th centuries are really indications of playing methods – not graphic representations of the work.

These diagrams show the precise positioning of the fingers necessary to produce the required chords (on a lute for example), in such a way that the music comes into existence when the notes are sounded. When one examines a fingering diagram, one cannot imagine the sounds produced, one sees only the positions. This is an extreme case of

Facsimile of a score by François Couperin

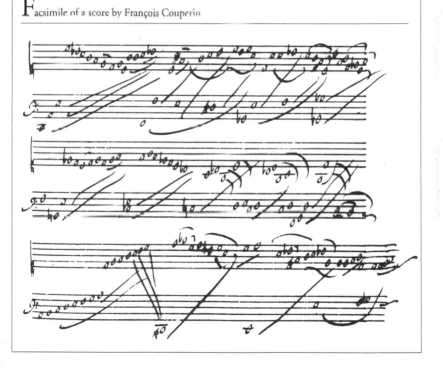

notation in the sense of an indication of playing method.

In compositions dating from after 1800 (the works of [Hector] Berlioz or Richard Strauss, for example, and many others) the aspect that is indicated as precisely as possible is how what is written should sound; only with a precise execution of the notes, paying careful attention to all instructions, can the correct music be produced.

If, on the other hand, we wish to play music that has been transcribed according to the principle of what we have called the *work*, i.e. music written before about 1800, we have no exact method for doing this. To discover it we must look elsewhere.

Clearly this also raises an important problem in teaching music, since one first learns the notation and only then is one taught to give shape to the music.

This supposes that standard notation means the same thing to all music, and no one tells a student that music written before about 1800 should be read differently from that written after this date. Teachers and pupils alike can be unaware of the fact that in the one case they are dealing with a form of notation relating to the playing of the piece, and in the other with a total composition, a work transcribed in a fundamentally different way.

These two alternative ways of reading a single form of notation – the transcription of the work and the

Contemporary notation: (below) Boguslav Schäffer, *Azione a due;* (opposite, above) Robert Moran, *Four Visions;* (opposite, below) Karlheinz Stockhausen, *Elektronische Studie II.*

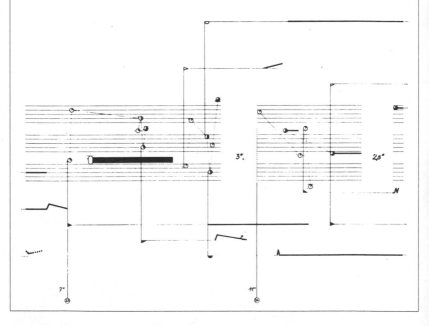

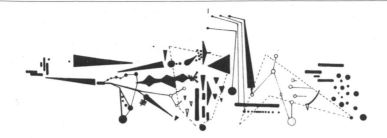

directions for playing – should be explained to all music students, both instrumental and vocal, at the beginning of their study of music theory. Otherwise they will sing or play in both cases 'what is written' (a common demand from music teachers), and therefore cannot do justice to the notation of the work without having analyzed it.

Possibly the best way to explain this is in terms of spelling. There is a form of musical orthography derived from musical treatises, musical theory and treatises on harmony. Certain peculiarities of musical notation result from this form of orthography; for

example the fact that the ritardandos, trills and appoggiaturas are not always written down – something that is aggravating if one believes that one has to play music 'as it is written'. Or the fact that the ornamentation is not fixed; writing it down would have hindered the creative imagination of the musician, which is precisely what is needed for free ornamentation.

Nikolaus Harnoncourt
The Musical Dialogue, 1984

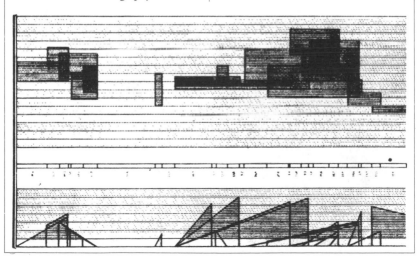

The influence of technique

With what and on what? These are the two questions that first spring to mind when one starts to consider the formation and evolution of writing, because, as much as on the civilizations that create them, written signs depend on the tools used to produce them and the medium on which they are written.

Runes: a plate taken from a 19th-century German work entitled *The Development of Writing.*

Leather, wax and silk

On what? On papyrus (Egypt), cloth (Egypt), tablets of baked clay (Mesopotamia), stone (Mesopotamia), marble (Greece), copper (India), leather (around the Dead Sea), deerskin (Mexico), birch bark (India), agave (Central America), bamboo (Polynesia), palm leaves (India), wood (Scandinavia), silk (China, Turkey), ivory (Autun), wax tablets (Egypt, Western Europe).

With what? Clearly, it is not possible to use the same instrument to write on all these different materials: reed stick, brush (made of papyrus or animal bristle), stylus and spatula, engraver, quill pen etc.

The medium and the instrument are the definers. It is easy to understand how two individuals in search of a writing system will conceive their signs in totally different ways depending on whether they are using a stick on papyrus or a stylus on clay. And even if, instead of inventing their own system of writing, they limit themselves to reproducing a

PERDVCANTALIOSTABVLAA
TVMCANITHESPERIDVMMI
TVMPHAETHONTIADASMV
CORTICISATQVESOLOPRO

M → M
G → G

LA POSITION DE L'OVTIL CHANGE
C'EST LA RVSTICA

known one, the result will still be quite different. After a certain length of time the nature of the medium will so condition the way the implement is used that all resemblance between the original and the reproduction will be lost.

I could have added the following to the list of materials used as media for writing: glass, bone, lead, iron, not forgetting parchment, vellum and, obviously, paper. The length of the list is unimportant. They did not all lead to innovation. This did not, however, prevent them from playing a significant role. Although the form of the signs was initially the result of the material and the tool, one must not lose sight of their subsequent development. When paper, for example, came into popular use, or when the position of the hand holding

the quill pen changed, the result was a change in style, even though this did not amount to a completely new system of writing.

Even the inexperienced eye can distinguish different scripts. What is very difficult to determine, on looking at a particular script, is the part that the medium played in it. One has to know whether a given material is the one on which the script originated, or one that later had an important modifying effect upon it.

All peoples have been seduced by the glory of stone inscriptions. Can we assume that writing which has come down to us in exclusively epigraphic form was never used in any other way? Could it not be that this form of writing represented the occasional adaptation of

L'ONOTO est l'arme moderne
dans la lutte des affaires

Advertising poster for the ONOTO pen, 1911.

a style of writing that the scribes would ordinarily have executed in some other medium that has not come down to us? This is the sort of information that one needs in order to understand why certain languages and writing systems have disappeared without trace, or have left only the slightest remains, whereas others, protected from the rigours of time, favoured by climate and recorded on less perishable materials, have survived more or less intact to the present day.

René Ponot
Communication and Language, 1973

The Romans made stone speak through their invention of the 'capitalis monumentalis' script. A model of sobriety and graphic purity, the beauty of the lapidary letter resides in a principle as simple as it is inspired: a stroke of shade, a flash of light. The Roman capital is at the same time the hallmark of a civilization and the consequence of a technique.

Of light and shade

What do we see if we compare the Greek inscriptions with the Latin inscriptions of the 3rd, 2nd and even 1st centuries? They are all of modest size – some few centimetres high – and consist of lines of equal weight. In other words, they are lineal inscriptions. The only difference that arises between the one and the other, from the oldest to the most recent, lies in the spirit of the line. The Greek capitals are geometric, with letters all designed on the same module; they reflect the need for order and method, and seem to embody the harmonious aspect of ancient Greek society. The Latin capital, more uncoordinated to begin with, sought initially to achieve a kind of unity from which it later strayed, varying the volume of the letters according to the morphology of each, favouring rhythm over cadence – a reflection of temperament. But this is the point where variations of thickness begin to appear, coinciding with the time when the Romans scattered monuments throughout their conquered territories to proclaim their great victories.

The inscriptions, which were no longer at eye-level, became therefore larger and more deeply cut into the stone. Even when tinted with colour, the grooves of the letters were rendered legible through the use of light and shade cast at different angles onto the lines. Rainwater gradually removed the colour

An inscription on Trajan's Column, the supreme achievement of Roman epigraphy.

from the vertical parts, leaving these less easily visible, while at the same time the horizontal lines became more pronounced as they caught and retained dirt, which emphasized the effect of the shadow.

If the letters were to retain their uniform appearance some alterations in their proportions had to be made. This was only possible by making the horizontal lines thinner than the verticals. It was also necessary to make the curves broaden as they approached the vertical and narrow as they curved away. This was a technique of 'writing with shadows'. No one can deny that aesthetics entered into this process. How else can one explain that the two verticals of the N – to take but one example – are thinner than the oblique that joins them? A reed is no more capable of producing a thick stroke and two thin strokes without altering the angle of the hand. But who would dare to attribute the evolution of a particular form to a single factor, no matter what it be or where it be found? In any case, it is technical considerations that determined the result, although one always has to allow for cases where the writer has deliberately introduced difficulties for himself – which is also often the case.

René Ponot
Of Lead, Ink and Light, 1982

Calligraphy and games with letters

Etymologically speaking, calligraphy means 'beautiful writing'. In practical terms, it forms a fragile, unfixed barrier between art and the needs of expression, between drawing and the writing of signs. For all time and in all places, wherever writing has existed, there has been an art of beautiful script and generally also groups of people, engravers or copyists, to execute it.

Calligram by Guillaume Apollinaire, 9 February 1915.

There are two main reasons why it was necessary to wait for Apollinaire for calligrams, until then referred to as 'figured verse', to be given their true name in the Graeco-Latin world.

Firstly, because in contrast to Hebrew and Arabic scripts – which are both in a sense calligrams – or even Chinese ideograms, whose origins lie in pictograms that can still partly be discerned, our Western writing systems do not lend themselves to calligraphic writing.

Western scripts are restrained by a tight bridle that prevents them from moving too freely. Now and again figured verses were able (in however limited a way) to break free and assume forms that were virtually those of nature. Beyond that they were, if not actually outlawed, then at least condemned as mere games that should not be boasted about. This is all the more difficult to understand because, even if such figured verses are in effect literary oddities, they require just as much skill in their production.

It was as if the Western scripts, and particularly Latin, were quite satisfied with themselves and preferred not to risk compromising what had been achieved through abstraction.

What was true of the Latin characters was even more so of Greek. This had developed earlier, and there was therefore an even greater risk of compromising a balance so dearly bought. The Greeks were not like the Arabs, whose writing not only lent itself to calligrammatic constructions, but indeed lay half-way between picture and script. In the Arab world, since man speaks in images, he identifies directly with his writing.

It would seem that for a long time man did not appreciate the full potential of figured verse, and considered it as just

Easter Wings

LORD, who createdst man in wealth and store,
Though foolishly he lost the same,
Decaying   more   and   more,
Till   he   became
Most poore:
With   thee
O   let   me   rise
As   larks,   harmoniously,
And   sing   this   day   thy   victories:
Then   shall   the   fall   further   the   flight   in   me.

My   tender   age   in   sorrow   did   beginne:
And   still   with   sicknesses   and   shame
Thou   didst   so   punish   sinne,
That   I   became
Most thinne.
With   thee
Let   me   combine,
And   feel this day thy victorie:
For, if I imp   my   wing   on   thine,
Affliction   shall   advance   the   flight   in   me.

George Herbert's poem *Easter Wings* of 1633.

another way of expressing himself. Even before reading the words, the reader knows effectively whether the text relates to the subject of wings, an egg or a political emblem. All the same, the poems of Simmias of Rhodes, the first known author of rhyming verse, who probably came from Symi, a small island off the north-east coast of Rhodes, and who lived in 300 BC under Ptolemy I, are all more cleverly constructed than they at first appear.

Simmias did not confine himself to giving his poems added visual appeal. He also tried to harmonize the rhythm of his verses with the figures that he intended to illustrate. The very shape of a pair of wings, of an egg or an axe, each suggested a form of versification appropriate to the subject itself. Here, the graphic and poetic forms (if I may be excused the pun on the word 'form', which is, in

these circumstances, inevitable) are so intricately linked that it would not be possible to use the one without finding the exact appropriate form of the other.

And so it was that, through the first efforts to produce calligrams, thought returned to the cradle of form. One senses that, subconsciously, there is a somewhat confused, but definite feeling that calligrams involve a search for a basis in reason not only of poetry but of language itself.

Jérôme Peignot
On Calligrams, 1980

Labyrinth, a calligraphic *tour de force* taken from a German treatise on the 'art of writing' dated to 1736.

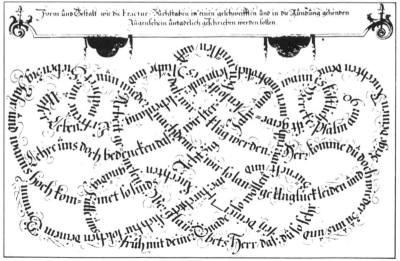

'It is more valuable to write books than to plant vines, since he who plants a vine feeds his stomach, while he who writes a book feeds his soul.' Thus wrote Alcuin, an English monk who reformed the art of calligraphy under Charlemagne. The advice of Paillasson, a French writing teacher of the 18th century seems charmingly old-fashioned. Nevertheless, the intellectual strength and physical discipline it requires have meant that the art of writing has remained a living art throughout many centuries and in many continents.

On general aptitude
There are those in whom the talent for writing seems to be inborn; with good will and consistent work such people will, in a short time, make appreciable progress in this art. There are others who, on the contrary, show no natural ability in this area. The latter have to struggle with their slower nature, which they will only succeed in defeating through exercise and practice. They will need more time than the former to arrive at the same stage. But are they not well rewarded by the advantage that they gain?

On the upstrokes, downstrokes and ligatures
Knowledge of the effects of the pen depends on a clear understanding of the distinction between the upstrokes, the downstrokes and the linking strokes, or ligatures. Downstroke refers to any mark not produced by the sharp edge of the pen, regardless of the direction in which this stroke is formed. The stroke we call the upstroke is the finest line that the pen can produce. The linking strokes are all the fine lines that join one letter to the next.

It is easy to see that the upstrokes and the links are not the same thing. Masters

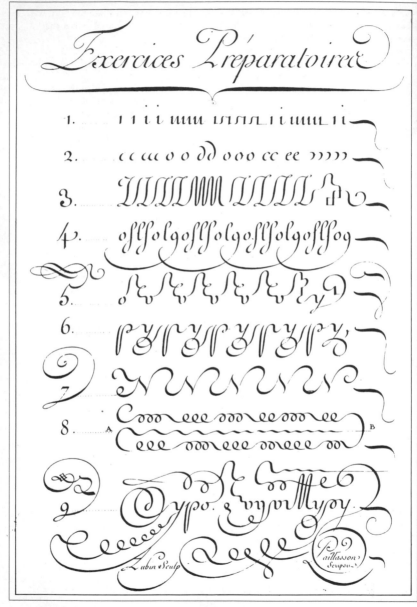

of the art distinguish between them by considering the upstroke to be part of the letter itself, whereas the link only serves to begin the letter, or to finish it, or to join it to another. The links in handwriting should not be neglected; they are to this art as the soul is to the body. Without these links there would be no movement, no fire, none of the vitality that lends quality to handwriting.

All the links and some of the upstrokes are produced by the action of the thumb and by the angled edge of the pen, which is also controlled by the thumb. Since this edge is heavily used in the construction of letters, it is made the longest and widest when cutting the pen. Following my principle, all links that are curved are more graceful than those lines produced by a diagonal.

There are all sorts of links, from round to vertical, from vertical to round, from round to round, vertical to vertical, base to top and many others that can be observed in examples of handwriting and in linked alphabets.

On the movement of the hand when writing

Speed in writing comes with time and practice. A hand that is new to writing must not attempt to hurry; neither, however, must it work too slowly. Both these contrasting faults produce equally undesirable effects. Excessive speed results in unprincipled and unbalanced writing; excessive slowness leads to heavy, tentative and sometimes shaky writing. Therefore a happy medium somewhere between the two extremes should be sought. When a hand that is familiar with the basics has reached a certain stage of perfection, it can gradually increase the speed at which it works, and begin to acquire the freedom that is necessary for all those destined for this work.

On form

The beautiful form of any writing is dependent on an exact observation of the rules and on sustained work. It is acquired through practising the letters on an enlarged scale and through an exact knowledge of the angles of the pen; this knowledge must be so familiar to the writer that he can produce any variation with his pen instinctively, without recourse to books or other information. I must also say on the subject of form that the writer should be very sure of it before passing on to more rapid writing, since any error that he makes when writing slowly and deliberately will be all the more glaringly obvious when he comes to write at greater speed.

On the touch of the pen

It is necessary to distinguish between two types of touch: the one that is a natural gift, and the one that is acquired by the exercise of the art. The natural touch is the truly significant one; it gives the ability to render things in a manner that appears both in the areas that have been touched by the pen and those that have been left untouched. One can be a competent writer without possessing this treasure. Nature does not bestow its gifts on everyone. The acquired touch does not have the same delicacy; it can be acquired by practice and a lightness of the hand, and by the style of cutting the nib, and the method of holding it with varying degrees of firmness. What should be looked for overall in the touch is the gentleness and softness that are so

distinctive effect. Taste examines, arranges and ensures that this effect should not be displeasing to the eye.

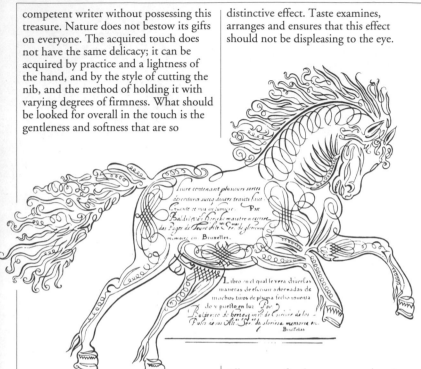

admired in writing, as opposed to the firmness and heaviness found in engraved characters, which are therefore less desirable.

On order in writing

If one knows how to write according to the rules but does not have an ordered mind, one only possesses part of the art. In order to acquire this quality it is necessary, as I have remarked on numerous occasions, to possess both imagination and taste. Imagination embellishes, enhances and provides a

All aspects of order are summed up in these few words. Thus any person who possesses these talents will be sure to produce a work that is far more regular than someone who lacks them. The former's work will be consistent, well-structured, correct in its spacing of words and lines, carefully considered in the choice of letters and free from that element of excess that almost invariably results in a visual impression of disorder and irregularity.

Paillasson
The Art of Writing, 1763

Turkish calligraphy dating to 1575 meaning 'In the name of Allah the merciful, the forgiving'.

It is among the Muslims, whose religion forbids representation of the human figure, that calligraphy has reached its apogee, because all the artist's efforts are concentrated in this particular area.

Content

The meaning of a text is one thing and its calligraphy quite another, but on occasion they are closely linked. Calligraphy does not consist solely in the creation of a text, but also of a composition that expresses an abstract concept of the world in general.

The relation between the blackness of the letters and the whiteness of the space around them should be studied in detail. Traditional calligraphy, understanding its art to perfection, can produce powerful compositions, full of emotion and ideas, which transmit the true meaning of the written word. Anyone who views a calligraphic work will respond first to the design of the writing and only then to the sense of the words. On occasion the sense may even be confused by the aesthetic effect of the script.

The calligraphic dimension is created by the richness and variety of the levels of perception: the overall composition, followed by the weighting of the black and white areas, the rhythm, and then the decipherment, first of the words themselves and then of the underlying meaning of the calligraphic form.

Turkish Kufic calligraphy meaning 'There is no God but God, and Mohammed is the messenger of God'.

Preparation

To the 20th century, the age of speed and profitability, calligraphy remains an expression of patience, wherein it is impossible to cut corners. The practice of calligraphy requires many years of

The name of Allah. The different aspects of Allah are written in small characters within the body of the letters.

apprenticeship and the assimilation of all aspects of culture that relate to it. It is necessary to produce exercises by copying the great masters; the discovery of the riches that they can offer will contribute to the refinement of an aesthetic vision.

A fruit tree develops slowly, drawing from the earth the nourishment that ripens its fruits and gives to each one its flavour, colour and scent. So also must the calligrapher ripen his art. Practice awakens the knowledge gradually stored up within his body, and releases the expression of myriad nuances.

Both acquired knowledge and spiritual preparation guide the calligrapher, concentrating and converging on the tip of his pen; from there is born the point, the stroke, the word, appearing from the ink like blood from his veins. The essence of the calligrapher becomes

totally dissolved in the ink, so that it can emerge from the tip of the quill.

Breath

The capacity of the calligrapher to hold his breath is reflected in the movement of his hand.... Normally one breathes instinctively. In the course of his apprenticeship the calligrapher learns to control his breathing and to profit by a break in the drawing of a letter to take a new breath.

A push or pull movement is altered according to whether the writer breathes in or out while making it. When the movement is long, the calligrapher holds his breath in order that the process of breathing should not interrupt its flow. Before calligraphing a letter or a word, he should note the spaces where it will be possible to take a breath and at the same

A composition in the style of Jeli Diwani de Hachem, 1957.

time to re-ink the pen. These breaks are made at very specific points in the text, even if it is possible to hold one's breath for longer or if there is still any ink remaining in the pen. The halts therefore serve to replenish both air and ink.

Calligraphers who choose to use traditional methods of writing do not like fountain pens, since these allow an uninterrupted flow of ink; mastery of breathing therefore becomes unnecessary, and the calligrapher loses the satisfaction of feeling the weight of time in his work.

Concentration
The moment when the calligrapher achieves total concentration represents the beginning of a transport of energy that will help him to overcome all oppressive difficulties. He will seek, in the deepest part of himself, his true path.

His whole body must participate in the calligraphic process and must function in harmony with his spirit. Total concentration requires an auditory and visual vacuum. The calligrapher must create a serene atmosphere, and his time must not be restricted by the constraints of everyday life. He will create a vacuum as if everything had disappeared from his surroundings. It will become a spherical vacuum of which he will be the centre, and the more his concentration increases, the nearer he will come to the true centre. Thus he will discover a rich world, of which he will be the master. His body will become weightless, his hand will grow wings, while his mode of expression will become more profound and truer to himself. His inner energy will reach a climax that will be conveyed to his writing.

Concentration provides an opening into a clearer and more lucid vision.

Beyond the rules

Calligraphic codes are the guardians of tradition, the link between different generations of calligraphers. There is no doubt that they can vary from one country to another and from one master to another. These codes serve to control the internal excitement of the calligrapher, and to prevent his feelings from overflowing. They arouse passionate debates between different calligraphers.

Their system of measurement provides an ideal reference point. But the calligrapher must pass beyond these set rules. In order to achieve his aim he must first conform to these restrictions, and then go beyond them. This is because a true calligraphic composition must contain something indefinable, intangible, something powerful that takes it beyond all rules.

Spacing

In a calligraphic composition there is no such thing as a blank space; there is only black and white, and each space, whether it be white or black has its own value. One can draw a comparison between architecture and calligraphy. An architectural design defines a living space, the space between the walls is as real and as significant as the walls themselves. In calligraphy the value of a space derives from its relationship with the letters that surround it, and vice versa.

Two distinct forms of calligraphy: (opposite, above) Baghdad calligraphy, 1952; (opposite, below) Thoulti mirror writing, from Rassa, 1903.

Expression

Joy, happiness, peace, anxiety and social violence are assimilated and expressed in the art of calligraphy. Through its capacity to absorb emotions and to revitalize them, it becomes a universal language, even though it is based on the Arabic alphabet and is therefore indecipherable for many....

The calligrapher identifies entirely with his art. He flies with the lightness

of one letter; he is bowed down by the weight of another. For him the achievement of expression represents a great moment of liberty. He cries what he has to say in an outpouring of words.

Calligraphic works reproducing material from past eras without changing the style of the composition remain on the margins of our own age. Those texts from ancient monuments, though innovative and fertile in their time, no longer speak to us in the same fashion. To each age its own vision.

Hassan Massoudy
Calligraphy, 1986

The art of writing in China

The mysterious essence of a work, be it painted, drawn or written, derives as much from the materials used to reproduce it, as from the matter it is intended to express. Chinese and Japanese writing are so closely linked, in the evolution of their techniques and media, as to be virtually inseparable.

Origins: Chai Lun and his discovery
Chai Lun was a functionary at the Han court (AD 25–220). To him is attributed the invention, in AD 107, of a light material, made by the crushing of vegetable fibres and their subsequent pressing into sheets....

It seems likely that Chai Lun's true achievement was to utilize and make known a process that was already common among certain artisans of the time, involving the recovery of hemp fibres which came from the recycling of old rags.

The first paste ever used to make paper in China was apparently produced from the fibres of used textiles, which were ground down and then moulded into fine sheets – a recycling of materials in which silk doubtless played a significant part. It was only after this

The Chinese character for brush.

that vegetable fibres came to be used on their own in the production of what was to become the paper of today.

Chai Lun's contribution was to discover new materials (old fishing nets, bark etc.) that could be used in a process that was already well known in his time, and then to present the results of using these materials to the authorities. Following this discovery, use of the new material spread rapidly throughout the country.

History: The Paper Road

Around AD 750 the Arab conquerors at Samarkand would have learned from Chinese prisoners the process for making paper from silk rags.

Until then the secret of this process had been jealously guarded by the Chinese, despite the fact that around AD 600 this knowledge had begun to spread east into Korea, and then to Japan, where it rapidly became established.

As for the dark paper made in Mexico by the Maya, and more recently by the Otomi Indians, this must be the result of the migration of proto-Mongolian peoples through the Bering Straits and along the Pacific Coast.

Thus the Paper Road was slowly drawn around the world. Towards the west, gradually, from Samarkand it took the route that was later to become known as the Silk Road, after the material that was usually transported along it: from Central Asia to Persia, Egypt, North Africa, and then to Spain, where the first paper-making centre was established in 1154, one thousand years after the first known discovery by Chai Lun.

Wood engravings showing the traditional method for making *washi*, Japanese paper.

As it made its way west the paper manufacturing process underwent numerous changes. Silk, which became too expensive even for re-use, was completely abandoned (even by the Chinese) in favour of scraps of hemp, cotton or linen, and it was in this form that paper came , via the Muslim world and after passing through many stages of development, to Europe, where it was known for several centuries as 'rag' paper.

The origins of ink in China

Unlike other aspects of writing, it is difficult to establish when ink first appeared in history.

The Chinese chronicles give it a legendary beginning, in attributing its invention to Tian Zhen, who lived under the mythical rule of Huang Di, the Yellow Emperor. This effectively hides the truth of the origins of this material. The era of Huang Di was also said to be the time when Chinese characters first came into existence.

The theoretical principles of manufacture

The principle of using an alloy of glue and soot to produce ink is in itself a very simple concept. It would be sufficient to produce, in the same way as any other coloured substance, a black liquid, soluble in water and usable in writing and painting.

But how does one progress from this to the qualities possessed by the best inks – their stability, their hardness, their deep, lustrous, slightly bluish colour? The requirements of calligraphers and then painters set a difficult task for the ink makers. There are endless treatises written on the subject of ink and its

The method for drying blocks of Chinese ink.

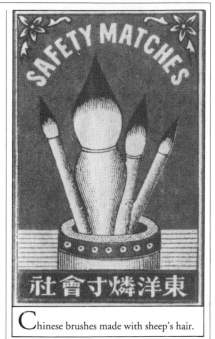

Chinese brushes made with sheep's hair.

manufacture, and it is not easy to extract from them a single ideal theory.

A note on Western 'Indian' ink
The ink found in China – a virtually indelible substance once it has undergone the high humidity treatment required by the mounting of Chinese paintings – is remarkably stable.

The only Indian aspect of the ink sold by European suppliers, and known as 'Indian' ink, is its name. It is called Indian ink because of its indelibility, which is produced by the presence of resin in its binder. It is much used throughout various branches of graphic art (drawing, wash drawing, musical scripts, plan drawing etc.). The composition of this ink, which varies depending on the nature of the resin used, is therefore different from true Chinese ink.

As for ordinary inks, such as those designed for use in fountain pens, it is not recommended that they be used on Oriental papers. The fugitive nature of the ink means that it will disappear at the slightest trace of humidity absorbed by the medium on which it is being used. The Japanese use the English term 'ink' to refer to all such unstable products; ink blocks are referred to by their Chinese name, pronounced by them as *sumi*.

The tip

For a calligrapher a good brush tip is essential. Every mark must be produced by using the central point of the brush. Lines produced with the flattened edge of the brush are to be avoided, although they are often simpler to produce; they

Three handwritten signs by the great scholar of the Sung dynasty, Mi Fei.

ruin the tip of the brush, making it necessary to replace the brush in the ink in order to restore its point, and the soft and ill-defined aspect created by these strokes detracts from the vitality and flow of the script.

Modern brushes are made according to the principle of a 'shaft' and 'mantle'. The empty space created between the two elements once the brush has been assembled forms a kind of reservoir, which functions rather like the cartridge of a fountain pen.

In the collection of Shosoin of Nara there are some especially tiny brushes dating to the 8th century AD. These have a paper paste core surrounded by long bristles, which form an extremely fine point. They were probably used for the writing of very small characters, where only the point of the brush would have been used.

As early as the 8th century, then, one can detect a preoccupation with avoiding the need to re-ink the brush too often, thereby retaining the correct breathing, which remains the most important aspect of good calligraphy. This preoccupation is reflected in the forerunner of the felt-tipped pen, which is, let us not forget, a Japanese invention.

The calligrapher's tool

Chinese writing could now take the breath that it had been holding for so many centuries. Under the Han dynasty the new opportunities offered by the use of the brush found expression in painting.

In frescoes (where the necessity of painting on a wet ground made second thoughts impossible) painting with a brush produced features that were more than simple lines; they represented true elements of expression. For a long time the line had a preparatory function when painting on silk or paper. In a rough carbon sketch a fine, even line discreetly surrounded the figure into which colour would later be placed.

Calligraphy underwent a tremendous expansion under the Chin dynasty (265–419) with the development of regular and cursive script. Under the Tang dynasty (618–907) the small, short-headed brush finally gave way to the long cone of soft bristles that so vividly produces the characteristic sweep of Chinese characters.

It was as a result of these innovations and the success with which they met that the free calligraphic line found a functional and expressive place in painting – a role that it has retained. The painting movement of the artists and writers of the Chan period served to reinforce its importance. Since then writing and painting have become inseparable.

Holding a brush

To dip a brush in the ink, to hold it vertically over a sheet of paper and draw a line takes only a few seconds. The difficulty involved in producing the desired line is rendered that much more agonizing by the knowledge that the absorbent capacity of paper or silk will make any repainting, correction or erasing quite impossible; in addition, the incredibly supple nature of the brush bristles means that any hesitation or shaking of the arm will appear in the line.

Claire Illouz
The Seven Treasures of the Learned, 1985

Ink painting of a bamboo branch, 18th century.

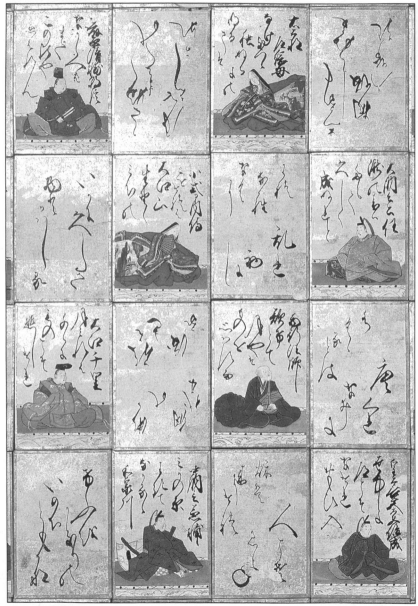

The pleasure of paper, of the hand, the weight of the arm resting on the table, the writing matching the movement that creates it: in 'The Empire of Signs' Roland Barthes expresses the essential aspects of Japanese writing and, on a more general level, all writing.

It is through stationery – the medium or support on which one writes and the range of tools necessary for writing – that one enters the world of signs; through stationery the hand encounters the instruments and materials necessary for the production of lines and marks; it is through stationery that we enter into the commerce of signs, even before they have been drawn. Every nation has its own style of stationery. That of the United States is abundant, precise and ingenious; it is the stationery of architects and students, where any exchange of signs assumes the relaxed postures of the participants; the stationery reveals that the user feels no need to invest anything of himself in his writing, but that he needs all the relevant commodities in order to translate into signs with ease the products of memory, of reading, of teaching and of communication.... French stationery, often purchased in 'Firms founded in 18..', with their black marble plaques encrusted with gold letters, remains a stationery of accountants, scribes and tradesmen; its typical product is the minute, the handwritten legal document, and its patrons are the eternal copyists, [Gustave Flaubert's] Bouvard and Pécuchet.

Japanese stationery is destined for that ideographic writing that appears to us to derive from painting, whereas painting actually derives from it. (It is important that art should start from writing, and from expression.) In as much as Japanese stationery creates forms and qualities for the two fundamental materials, that is, the surface and the writing instrument, so it neglects – comparatively – those chance aspects of recording that give American stationery its extraordinary imaginative luxury. Its line excludes all possibility of erasure or repetition (since the character is drawn *alla prima*); there is no equivalent invention to the eraser or its substitutes (the eraser, an object that symbolizes the line we would like to remove, or at least to lighten or narrow...). All aspects of the tools are geared towards the production of writing that is paradoxical, at once irreversible and incredibly fragile, which, though it glides over the paper, has as unalterable an effect as if it were cut into it: thousands of types of paper, in many of which it is possible to discern in the fine grain of the sheet their origins as light-coloured straw or crushed blades of grass; notebooks, whose pages are folded in two like those of an uncut book, so that the writing spreads across a luxurious surface unaware of the spreading stain of the ink, the metonymical impregnation of the obverse and reverse (writing is done over an empty space): the palimpsest, the line that is erased and thereby becomes a secret, is an impossibility. As for the brush (inked by rubbing it gently over a lightly moistened ink block), it has its

Japanese literary game from the 19th century: verses by the hundred most celebrated Japanese poets.

own gestures, as does a finger; but where our ancient quills could produce only the wider and finer strokes of a script, and could only scratch away at the paper in one direction, the brush has a freedom of movement, allowing it to glide, jump and twist across the paper – the mark being created in the air, as it were, with the fleshly, lubricated flexibility of the hand. The felt-tipped pen, of Japanese origin, has taken over from the brush; this type of pen is not an improvement on the nibbed pen, itself a product of the quill (steel or feather); its direct heredity is that of the ideogram. This graphic style of thought, to which all Japanese stationery is related (in each large Japanese store there is a public scribe whose job it is to write in vertical columns on long, red-bordered envelopes the addresses to which presents are being sent), is to be found, paradoxically (at least for us), in everything – right up to the typewriter.

Our typewriters aim to turn writing into an almost mercenary product, pre-editing the text as it is written; the Japanese typewriter, with its innumerable characters, not aligned in a single keyboard but placed in rolls on drums, is reminiscent of drawing, an ideographic marquetry spread across the page – in a word, space. In this way the machine perpetuates a true graphic art that does not derive from the aesthetic production of a single letter, but from the abolition of the sign, scattered headlong across the page in every possible direction.

Roland Barthes
The Empire of Signs, 1970

Opposite: Japanese print showing the teaching of writing, 19th century.

Chinese poems.

Approximately one-fifth of the world's population uses writing systems that are ideographic rather than alphabetic. Whether this is seen as a cause or effect, these writing systems mirror correspondingly different social and psychological systems.

The Chinese writing system has not developed into a phonetic representation of the language, and it has therefore never been possible to see it in any way as a reproduction of the spoken word; it is probably for this reason that the written sign, a symbol as unique as that which it represents, has retained so much of its primitive prestige. There is no reason to believe that in ancient China the spoken word was not as effective as the written word, but its strength may have been partially eclipsed by the power of the written symbol. In contrast, in civilizations where writing evolved fairly early into a syllabary or alphabet, it was the spoken word that absorbed all the power of magical and religious creation. In fact, it is remarkable that this astonishing emphasis on the value of the spoken word, the syllable and the vowel, which is attested in all the major

A Korean calligraphy master.

civilizations from the Mediterranean basin through to India, is not to be found in China.

Chinese written characters are individualized in order to serve as immediate marks (marks of power, identifying marks, indications of ownership or manufacture); Chinese seals regularly have characters on them. This is not true of the West or the Near East, where seals usually have a drawing on them. Syllabaries and alphabets have meant that written characters have become too uniform to be used as identifying marks. Above all, no single sign represents a unique reality, since each one forms part of a composition using countless written words.

A written name in China can function as a substitute for any other representation of that person (a statue, for instance, or a drawing). Therefore, at the moment when a dead man's soul is about to enter his funerary tablet, the characters of his name are written on it. The gods that guard houses against the evil eye are represented sometimes by paintings and sometimes simply by their written name.

Finally, written signs in Chinese, as everyone knows, often serve as representations of wishes. Characters representing the desire for happiness, long life, success in a public career or wealth are reproduced in vast numbers on jewelry, clothing, furniture and many other varied objects. This particular form of symbolism is exclusive to China and is not found in any civilization where writing functions as a phonetic representation of the language.

Written characters in Chinese serve therefore as an expression of wishes, first, because they have a specific form that corresponds uniquely to the reality they are intended to evoke, and, second,

Chinese newspaper, c. 1890.

dialectic and even linguistic changes. The Japanese have borrowed all their graphic scientific vocabulary from the Chinese, despite the fact that their own language, with its polysyllabism and syntax, is so profoundly different from Chinese. This inheritance is so significant and so valuable, from both a semantic and an aesthetic point of view, that the Japanese have been unable to forgo it in favour of an alphabetic writing, which would, for them, produce the effect of a confused collection of sounds and shapes.

Even in China the continuation of these written forms from antiquity has had similar results: because the characters themselves have remained unchanged, they have amassed a large number of meanings. From this stems the difficulty to be found in reading Chinese literature – it is not so much the complexity of the writing system, which despite everything exists within a well-balanced system with its own logic, but more the multiplicity of meanings that come from different eras and different scribal usages.

The uninterrupted enrichment of the written language has resulted in the writing becoming a form of repository for all Chinese intellectual inheritance, thus reducing the spoken language to a very lowly role: that of expressing daily commonplaces. No doubt this goes a long way towards explaining both the part played by literature in Chinese civilization and that played by the well-read element of Chinese society.

Jacques Gernet
In *Writing and the Psychology of Peoples*, 1963

because of their aesthetic value and their ornamental function....

Whereas alphabetic writing systems are fairly closely linked to the changing reality of language, that which, on the contrary, makes spoken Chinese – and also the written Chinese language – a remarkable instrument of civilization is its independence of phonetic evolution,

*At the time of his travels in Asia in
1930–1, the Belgian poet and painter
Henri Michaux encountered ideographic
Chinese writing and was left with the
sensation that he was little more than a
barbarian.*

In the creation of Chinese characters,
what is most striking is the lack of feeling
for the solid whole, or for spontaneity,
and the preference for using one detail to
signify the whole. As a result the Chinese
language, which could have become
universal, has never crossed the Chinese
border, except in the case of Korea and
Japan, and is considered the most
difficult language to learn.

There are not even five characters in
twenty thousand that can be understood
on first sight, unlike Egyptian
hieroglyphs, whose separate elements, if
not the whole, are easily recognizable....

The Chinese have a passion for
combinations. Let us consider an
example that would seem fairly
straightforward: a chair. In Chinese it is
written using the following elements
(which are in themselves unrecognizable): 1) tree; 2) large; 3) sighing with
pleasure and admiration. The whole
means *chair*, and is very likely composed
as follows: a man (squatting on his heels
or standing), sighing with pleasure near
an object made from the wood of a tree.
Even if one could identify the different
elements it would help! But if you do not
know in advance what you are looking
for, you will not find them.

The idea of representing the chair
itself with its seat and its legs does not
occur to them. The Chinese have found
the chair that suits them, unobvious,
discreet, subtly suggested by elements
from the world around them, formed as a
mental deduction rather than represented
– and yet uncertain, merely hinted at.

*M*ovements by Henri Michaux, 1951.

This particular character... shows clearly how much the Chinese dislike the sight of an object in its raw state, and how in contrast their taste veers towards combinations and figurative representations. Even if they begin by representing an object as it appears, after a short while it tends to be distorted and simplified.

For example, over the centuries the elephant has taken on eight different shapes. Originally, it had a trunk. Several

centuries later it still has one. But in the meantime the poor animal was made to stand upright like a man. Some time afterwards it lost its eye and its head; still later the body disappeared, leaving only the feet, the spinal column and the shoulders. Later it recovered its head but lost everything else except the feet; and later still it became twisted into the form of a snake. Finally it became whatever you like: it has two horns and a teat emerging from a foot.

Henri Michaux
A Barbarian in Asia, 1933

Alpha, Beta and others

Among the many achievements of the 'Encyclopédie', 1751–75, was that it provided the first scholarly account of the writing systems of the world. These extracts appeared in the volume 'L'Art d'écrire' of 1763. Diderot's eccentric spellings of Arabic names have been left as he wrote them.

Diderot and D'Alembert's introduction to the volume 'L'Art d'écrire' of the *Encyclopédie*

We flatter ourselves that the public will welcome the collection of ancient and modern alphabets that we present here. It is neither as full nor as detailed as we would have wished, but we can at least guarantee that it is more accurate than anything of this kind that has appeared hitherto.

We have taken particular care to transcribe these alphabets from the best original sources that we could find; often we have had several examples in front of us at the same time in order to guide our choice. Those to be found in large numbers in the publications of Duret and in other collections are badly executed and ill-chosen; many of them are completely false and imaginary. We hope that no one will be able to level the same reproach at us. We would rather content ourselves with a smaller number than risk including even one of which we were unsure.

Most of the Indian alphabets included in this collection were sent from Pondicherry at least thirty years ago. It was then intended, in a scheme prompted by certain rich Frenchmen, to have punches cut in Paris in order to set up several printing presses in India, following the example of the Danish, who already had a Tamil or Malabari press there. From this one may judge the accuracy of these alphabets and the degree of confidence to be placed in them.

Since all things should be governed by order, it is by no means unfitting that we should explain at this point the principles we have followed in arranging these alphabets.

We thought we should begin with Hebrew and the other alphabets that

ALPHABET GREC.

Figura		Nomen	
A	α	ἀλ φα	Alpha
B	ββ	βῆτα	Vita
Γ	γ	γάμμα	Gamma
Δ	ολδ	δἑλτα	Delta
E	ε	εψιλὸν	Epsilon
Z	ξ	ζῆτα	Zita
II	n	νἷα	Ita
⊖	θϑ	ᵶῆτα	Thita
I	ι	ιῶτα	Iota
K	κ	κάππα	Cappa
Λ	λ	λάμβδα	Lambda
M	μ	μῦ	My
N	ν	νῦ	Ny
Ξ	ξ	ξῖ	Xi
O	ο	ομικρὸν	Omicron
II	ϖ π	πῖ	Pi
P	ρ	ρῶ	Rho
Σ	σς	σιγμα	Sigma
T	τΤ	ταῦ	Tau
Υ	υ	υψιλὸν	Ypsilon
Φ	φ	φῖ	Phi
X	χ	χῖ	Chi
Ψ	ψ	ψῖ	Psi
Ω	ω	ωμέγα	Omega

derive from it, such as Samaritan, Syriac, Arabic, Egyptian, Phoenician, Palmyrian, Syro-Galilean and Ethiopian. From these we pass to the ancient Greek and Latin alphabets and to the various European alphabets which clearly derive from them.

Then come the Armenian, Georgian and ancient Persian alphabets, which seem to have no connection with the foregoing, either in the form of the characters or in their denominations. After that we place the Indian alphabets – Grantha, Sanskrit, Bengali, Telugu, Tamil, Siamese, Balinese, Tibetan, Manchurian Tartar and Japanese.

Finally, we conclude with Chinese characters. Chinese may challenge Hebrew and Samaritan in point of antiquity, but since it is essentially a pictographic writing system, and originally simply represented the objects signified, and consequently bears no relation to alphabetic characters, we felt justified in assigning it this position in the book, without in any way wishing to deny its claims to great antiquity, of which I am fully persuaded.

Plate VIII: The Greek alphabet

The Greek alphabet used here [left] is taken from an inscription from Sigeion, published in 1727 by the learned Mr Chishull. We have taken pains to reproduce the characters in the two ways in which they are written, that is, both from left to right and from right to left. This is how the *boustrophedon* inscriptions brought back by Monsieur l'Abbé Fourmont from his travels in Greece are arranged.

It is called *boustrophedon* because the Greeks who incised these inscriptions in marble were apparently undecided whether to adopt the convention of writing from left to right, or to keep to that of writing from right to left, which they had borrowed from the Phoenicians. Their solution was to employ both systems of writing at once, so that having written the first line from right to left, they wrote the next from left to right, and continued in this manner alternately, line by line, imitating the furrows made in a field by an ox ploughing, which is what the term *boustrophedon* means in Greek.

The oldest Arabic characters are called Kufic, after the town of Kufa, which was built on the Euphrates river. The characters that are in use today are the invention of the Vizier Moclah, who flourished in AD 933 under the Caliphs Moctader, Caher-Billah and Badhi-Biliah.

The intrigues of this vizier cost him at various times his right hand, his left hand and finally his tongue, reducing him to a life of misery and suffering which he ended in 949.

It is reported that when he was condemned to lose his right hand he complained that he was being treated as a common thief, and that they were depriving him of a hand that had made three copies of the Koran – copies which would serve as models of the most perfect writing for ever after.

Indeed, these copies have never ceased to be admired for the elegance of their characters, notwithstanding the fact that in the judgment of the Arabs they were later surpassed by Ebn-Bauvad. Others attribute the invention of these fine characters to Eba Moclah's brother, Abdallah-al-Hassan.

Some Kufic inscriptions still survive, which are extremely beautiful, but they tend to be rather difficult to read because of the extraneous ornament with which they are encrusted.

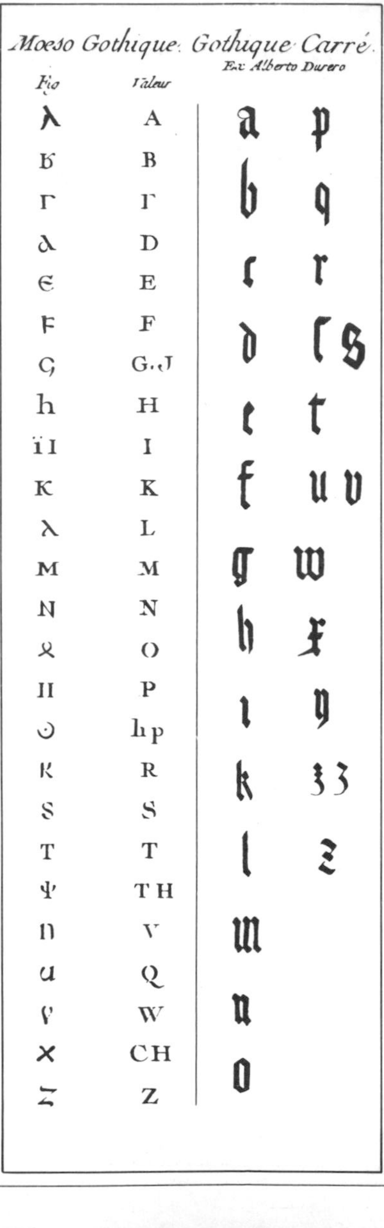

Moeso Gothique. Gothique Carré.
Ex: Alberto Durero

Fig	Valeur
λ	A
Ƀ	B
Γ	Γ
ꝺ	D
Є	E
Ϝ	F
Ɡ	G, J
h	H
ïI	I
Κ	K
λ	L
М	M
N	N
ꝍ	O
ΙΙ	P
ꝋ	h p
Ʀ	R
S	S
T	T
Ψ	T H
�	V
u	Q
Ƿ	W
Χ	CH
Ζ	Z

Plate IX: The Gothic alphabet

Writing was first introduced to the Goths by Ulphilas, a Goth by nationality, who was the successor of Theophilus as bishop of the Goths at the time of the Emperor Valens. Certain writers maintain, however, that Ulphilas did not actually invent the Gothic alphabet [left] himself; it was because he had used it for his translation of the Holy Scriptures from the Greek, they explain, that he was regarded as the originator of the characters.

Nevertheless, there is reason to think that the assertions of these writers are based on nothing but the imaginary antiquity with which they wish to endow Gothic letters. If we are to believe them, the Goths already had writing at a time before Carmenta came to Italy from Greece with Evander. They even push this antiquity beyond the Flood and as far as the age of the Giants, to whom they attribute the erection of those enormous piles of stones that are to be seen in the North.

These authors, in order to prove what they so lightly propose, would have to accord the same antiquity to Greek letters, since it is certain that Gothic letters are derived from them.

Plate X: The Russian alphabet

Historians of the late Roman empire assert that the Russians, or Muscovites, had no system of writing before the reign of the Byzantine emperor Michael the Paphlagonian, when they adopted the language and characters of the Slavs [right]; the characters were Greek. The Russians trace their origins to the Slavs, although their tsars believe themselves to be descended from the Romans; that is to say, from the emperors of Constantinople, who called themselves

Russe	Moderne	Russe	Ancien
А А а	Азъ	а̃ а̃зъ
Ꙩ Ꙩ σ	Буки	Б буки
В В в	Вѣдъ	Б вѣди
Г Г г	Глаголь	Г глаголь
Д Д д	Добро	Д добро
Е Е е	Есть	е̃ е є̃сть
Ж Ж ж	Живѣше	Ж живѣк'те
Ѕ Ѕ ѕ	Ѕѣло	Ѕ ѕѣлѡ
З З з	Земля	З земл̃а
И И и	Иже	И иже
І і іи	Иⷮ	ї ї
К К к	Како	к̃ ка́кѡ
Л Л л	Лю, ди	Л лю́ди
М М м	Мыслѣше	М мыслъ'те
П П п	Нашъ	Н нашъ
О О о	Онъ	Ѡ о́нъ
П П п	Покои	П покои
Р Р р	Рцы	р̃ рцы̃
С С с	Слово	с слово
Т Т т	Тверꙸдо	т̃ твёрꙷло
У У у	Ук	У У укъ
Ф Ф ф	Фертъ	ф фертъ
Х Х х	Хѣрь	Х х'кр'ъ
Ц Ц ц	Цы	ц цы̃
Ч Ч ч	Червь	ч чёрвь
Ш Ш ш	Ша	ш ша
Щ Щ щ	Ща	ψ ща
Ъ Ъ ъ	Еръ	ъ е̃р'ъ
Ы Ы ы	Еры	ы е̃ры̃
Ь Ь ь	Ерь	ь е̃рь
Ѣ Ѣ ѣ	Яшъ	ѣ и̃тъ
Э Э э	Э	Є
Ю Ю ю	Ю	ю̃ кси̃
Я Я я	Я	ѱ пси̃
Ѳ Ѳ ѳ	Ѳита	ѳ ѳи̃тъ
Ѵ Ѵ ѵ	Ѵжица	ѵ ижица

Ord.	Val.	Firo-Canna	Catta-Canna	Imatto-Canna
1	a	あ	ア	
2	je		エ	
3	i	い	イ	
4	o	を	ヲ	
5	u	う	ウ	
6	fa	は	ハ	
7	fe	へ	ヘ	
8	fi	ひ	ニ	
9	fo	ほ	ホ	
10	fu	ふ	ツ	
11	ka	か	カ	
12	ke	け	ケ	

Romans. Monsieur l'Abbé Girard of the Académie Française, who is well known for his excellent work *Des Synonymes* and for his French grammar, had before his death also composed a grammar and dictionary of Latin, French and Russian. Monsieur Le Breton, Printer in Ordinary to the King, the friend to whom he left all his manuscripts, presented this to the Russians several years ago, on the sole condition that they should give Monsieur l'Abbé Girard the credit that he and his work deserved.

Plate XXIV: Japanese alphabets

This plate [left] contains three different Japanese alphabets. The first, called *Firo-Canna,* and the second, *Catta-Canna,* are common to the Japanese in general, and in use among the people. The alphabet called *Imatto-Canna,* or rather *Jamatto-Canna,* is used only at the court of the Dairo, or hereditary religious emperor; it derives its name from the province of Jammasriro, where Miaco, the seat of the prince, is situated.

It is not difficult to see that the elements of these three alphabets come from Chinese characters. Indeed they are all Chinese characters, very freely drawn, but pronounced differently. Since each character stands for a complete syllable, it has inevitable disadvantages in comparison with our languages, where the alphabets, made up of single vowels and consonants, can express all kinds of sounds.

I do not know whether these alphabets predate the arrival of Europeans in Japan, or whether the Japanese invented them for themselves. Japanese scholars can read Chinese books as easily as the Chinese themselves, but the way they pronounce the same characters is very different. The Japanese can also write in Chinese; and often, to make reading easier, they interlineate the Chinese characters with their own characters. The Manchu Tartars do the same. I forgot to mention that, like the Chinese, they write vertically – from top to bottom – and from right to left.

Plate XXV: Chinese characters

The Chinese have no alphabet; their very language is incompatible with one, since it is made up of an extremely limited number of sounds. It would be impossible to convey the sound of Chinese through our alphabet, or any other alphabet. Chinese has only 328 vocables, all monosyllables, while there are roughly 80,000 characters, each standing for a word [below]. This would give an average of 243 or 244 characters for every monosyllable.

Now, if we are occasionally bothered by words in French that have different meanings but which sound and are written the same – and there are very few of these – imagine the endless confusion that the Chinese must have, trying to speak a language of which every word is capable of some 244 different meanings.

Denis Diderot and Jean D'Alembert
Encyclopédie, 1751–75

The day that man broke language down into sounds and invented graphic signs to represent these sounds, he bestowed upon humanity the greatest cultural tool one could ever dream of. Rudyard Kipling tells how Taffy, a young Neolithic girl, invented the 'wonderful old alphabet'.

How the Alphabet was made

Taffy took a marrow-bone and sat mousy-quiet for ten whole minutes, while her Daddy scratched on pieces of birch-bark with a shark's tooth. Then she said, 'Daddy, I've thinked of a secret surprise. You make a noise – any sort of noise.'

'Ah!' said Tegumai. 'Will that do to begin with?'

'Yes,' said Taffy. 'You look just like a carp-fish with its mouth open. Say it again please.'

'Ah! ah! ah!' said her Daddy. 'Don't be rude, my daughter.'

'I'm not meaning to be rude, really and truly,' said Taffy. 'It's part of my secret-surprise-think. *Do* say *ah*, Daddy, and keep your mouth open at the end, and lend me that tooth. I'm going to draw a carp-fish's mouth wide-open.'

'What for?' said her Daddy.

'Don't you see?' said Taffy, scratching away on the bark. 'That will be our little secret s'prise. When I draw a carp-fish with his mouth open in the smoke at the back of our Cave – if Mummy doesn't mind – it will remind you of that ah-noise. Then we can play that it was me jumped out of the dark and s'prised you with that noise – same as I did in the beaver-swamp last winter.'

'Really?' said her Daddy, in the voice that grown-ups use when they are truly attending. 'Go on, Taffy.'

'Oh, bother!' she said. 'I can't draw all of a carp-fish, but I can draw something that means a carp-fish's mouth. Don't you know how they stand on their heads rooting in the mud? Well, here's a pretence carp-fish (we can play that the rest of him is drawn). Here's just his mouth, and that means *ah*.'

And she drew this.

'That's not bad,' said Tegumai, and scratched on his own piece of bark for himself; 'but you've forgotten the feeler that hangs across his mouth.'

'But I can't draw, Daddy.'

'You needn't draw anything of him except just the opening of his mouth and the feeler across. Then we'll known he's a carp-fish, 'cause the perches and trouts haven't got feelers. Look here, Taffy.'

And he drew this.

'Now I'll copy it,' said Taffy. 'Will you understand *this* when you see it?'

And she drew this.

'Perfectly,' said her Daddy. 'And I'll be quite as s'prised when I see it anywhere as if you had jumped out from behind a tree and said "Ah!"'

Rudyard Kipling
Just So Stories, 1902

The 19th-century French novelist Victor Hugo was a lover of 'things that can be seen and understood', and he loved above all else the French language and the system used to compose it: the alphabet.

From the house of man to God

Have you ever noticed that the letter 'Y' is a picturesque letter open to countless different interpretations? A tree is in the shape of a 'Y', the fork of two roads forms a 'Y'; two rivers flow together in a 'Y'; the head of a donkey or that of an ox is in the shape of a 'Y'; the stem of a glass is 'Y'-shaped; a lily on its stalk is a 'Y'; a man who prays to the heavens raises his arms in the shape of a 'Y'.

Besides, this observation can be applied to all aspects of what constitutes basic human writing. All that is to be found in the demotic language is there because it was put there by hieratic. The hieroglyph is the essential root of the written character. All letters began as signs, and all signs began as images.

Human society, the world and the whole of mankind is to be found in the alphabet. Freemasonry, astronomy, philosophy, all the sciences find their true, albeit imperceptible beginnings there; and so it must be. The alphabet is a well-spring.

A is the roof, the gable with its cross-bar, the arch; or it is the greeting of two friends who embrace and shake hands; D is the back; B is D upon D, the back on the back, the hump; C is the crescent, the moon; E is the foundations, the pillar, the console and the architrave, the whole of architecture in a single letter; F is the gallows, the gibbet, *furca*; G is the French horn; H is the facade of a building with its two towers; I is a war machine launching its projectile; J is the ploughshare and the horn of plenty; K is the angle of reflection equal to the angle of incidence, one of the keys to geometry; L is the leg and the foot, M is a mountain or a camp where the tents are pitched in pairs; N is a gate closed by a diagonal bar; O is the sun; P is the porter standing with a burden on his back; Q is the rump and the tail; R represents rest, the porter leaning on his stick; S is the snake, T the hammer; U is the urn, V the vase (hence the two are often confused); I have already discussed Y; X is crossed swords, combat – Who will be the victor? We do not know – so the mystics adopted X as the sign of destiny, and algebraists chose it to represent the unknown; Z is lightning, it is God.

So, first man's house and his architecture, then his body, its structure and its weaknesses; then justice, music, the church; war, harvest and geometry; the mountains, nomadic life, cloistered life; astronomy; work and rest; the horse and the serpent; the hammer and the urn that can be upturned and strung up to make a bell; trees, rivers, roads; and finally destiny and God: that is what the alphabet contains.

Victor Hugo
Travel Notebooks, 1839

Writing

I have often asked myself why I enjoy writing (manually, that is), to such an extent that on occasion the vain effort of intellectual work is redeemed in my eyes by the pleasure of having in front of me (like some DIY workbench) a beautiful sheet of paper and a good pen: while thinking about what I should write (as is the case at this very moment), I feel my hand move, turn, join, dive and lift, and often, through the act of correction, delete or expand a line, taking the space right up to the margin, thus constructing from the apparently functional lines of the letters a space that is quite simply that of a work of art. I am an artist, not because I am representing an object, but, in a more basic sense, because in writing my body knows the joy of drawing on and rhythmically incising a virgin surface (its virginity representing the infinitely possible).

This particular pleasure must date back a very long way: on the walls of certain prehistoric caves series of evenly spaced incisions have been found. Were they already a form of writing? By no means.

Doubtless these marks meant nothing, but their very rhythm expresses a conscious activity, probably magic or, more broadly speaking, symbolic: the line, dominated, organized, sublimated (it mattered little how). The human desire to incise (with a stylus or a pen nib) or to caress (with the brush or felt pen) has certainly undergone many changes through the ages, which have combined to overshadow the true physical origin of writing; but it is sufficient that from time to time a painter (such as [André] Masson or [Cy] Twombly today) should incorporate graphic forms in his or her work, to make us reconsider the evidence. Writing is not only a technical process; it is also a joyous physical experience.

If I give this aspect a position of primary importance, it is because it is normally denied. That is not to say that the invention and the development of writing were not determined by the most imperious movement in history: social and economic history. It is well known that in the Mediterranean area (as

Today almost everybody can write – in our Western countries, that is. So has the history of writing come to an end? Have we no more to say on the subject?... It is too soon to say what aspect of himself modern man has invested in this new writing, in which the hand no longer plays any part. Surely, though, even if the hand is absent, the eye must still be involved. Man's body remains linked to

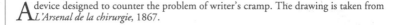

A device designed to counter the problem of writer's cramp. The drawing is taken from *L'Arsenal de la chirurgie*, 1867.

opposed to the Asiatic region), writing was born out of commercial needs; the development of agriculture, the need to establish records of stored grain, forced man to invent a means of noting down what was necessary for the functioning of the community, of discovering a method of recording that would control storage times and distribution space. From this writing was born – in the West, at least.

his writing by the vision that he has of it: there are typographical aesthetic values. There is therefore a use for any book that teaches us to distance ourselves from the text in the exercise of a simple reading and to see the letter, as the ancient calligraphers did, as an enigmatic projection of our own bodies.

Roland Barthes
Preface to *The Civilization of Writing*,
R. Druet and H.Grégoire, 1976

Contre-écriture by Roland Barthes.

FURTHER READING

THE HISTORY OF WRITING

Alleton, Viviane. *L'Ecriture chinoise.* 1980

Best, Jan G.P. *Ancient Scripts from Crete and Cyprus.* 1988

Chadwick, John. *Linear B and Related Scripts.* 1987

Claiborne, Robert. *The Miracle of Writing.* 1974

Cohen, Marcel. *La Grande Invention de l'écriture et son évolution.* 1958

Coulmas, Florian. *The Writing Systems of the World.* 1989

Döblhofer, E. *Le Déchiffrement des écritures.* 1959

Etiemble, René. *L'Ecriture.* 1978

Faulkner, Raymond O. *Book of the Dead.* Rev ed. 1985

Gaur, Albertine. *A History of Writing.* 1987

Goody, Jack. *The Logic of Writing and the Organization of Society.* 1986

Harris, Roy. *The Origin of Writing.* 1986

Houston, Stephen D. *Maya Glyphs.* 1989

Jackson, Donald. *The Story of Writing.* 1981

Katan, Norma J. *Hieroglyphs.* Rev. ed. 1985

Massin, Robert. *Letter and Image.* 1972

Nakanishi, Akira. *Writing Systems of the World.* 1980

Page, Raymond I. *Runes.* 1987

Quirke, Stephen, and Carol Andrews. *The Rosetta Stone: Facsimile Drawing with an Introduction and Translations.* 1989

Reading the Past: Ancient Writing from Cuneiform to the Alphabet. Intro. J.T. Hooker. 1990

WRITING AS ART

Bologna, Giulia. *Illuminated Manuscripts: The Book before Gutenberg.* 1988

Calkins, Robert G. *Illustrated Books of the Middle Ages.* 1983

Chalfont, Henry. *Spraycan Art.* 1987

Harthan, John. *Books of Hours and their Owners.* 1977

Henderson, George. *From Durrow to Kells: The Insular Gospel-books 650–800.* 1987

James, David. *Qur'ans of the Mamluks.* 1988

Peignot, Jérôme. *Du Calligramme.* 1978.

Massoudy, Hassan. *La Calligraphie arabe vivante.* 1981

Three Classics of Italian Calligraphy: Arrighi, Tagliente and Palatino. Intro. Oscar Ogg. 1953

Whalley, Joyce I., and Vera C. Kaden. *The Universal Penman: A Survey of Western Calligraphy from the Roman Period to 1980.* Catalogue of an exhibition at the Victoria and Albert Museum, London. 1980

TYPOGRAPHY AND PRINTING

Carter, Sebastian. *Twentieth-century Type Designers.* 1987

Harthan, John. *The History of the Illustrated Book: The Western Tradition.* 1981

Peignot, Jérôme. *De l'Ecriture à la typographie.* 1967

Updike, Daniel B. *Printing Types: Their History, Forms and Use.* 1980

LIST OF ILLUSTRATIONS

The following abbreviations have been used:
a above, *b* below, *l* left, *r* right.

COVER

Front: (Centre) Ru-Xiao-Fan. Chinese character for 'brush'. 20th century; (Anti-clockwise from bottom left) *The book-pedlar.* 16th-century wood engraving. Musée Carnavalet, Paris; Detail of a plate entitled 'L'Art d'écrire', from the *Encyclopédie,* D. Diderot and J. D'Alembert, 1763; Cover of a Kufic Koran from the Maghreb. Photograph; Hieroglyphic cartouche in *Voyage en Egypte,* J.-F. Champollion. Photograph
Spine: Verses by Ruteboeuf with illuminated capitals. 13th-century French manuscript. Bibliothèque Nationale (Bibl. Nat.), Paris
Back: Jean Gerson writing. 15th-century French manuscript. Bibl. Nat., Paris

OPENING

CHAPTER 1

Constructions des Lettres c *et* d.

PHOTO CREDITS

Ackermann 132. © ADAGP Paris, 1987 129, 141, 186-7. Bibliothèque Nationale 1, 2, 3, 4, 5, 6, 7, 47*l*, 48, 54-5, 55*b*, 56, 57, 63, 68*a*, 69, 74, 80, 82, 84, 86*b*, 87, 88, 89, 90, 91*l*, 92*bl*, 117, 118*b*, 119, 167*b*, 176. British Museum 76-7, 78-9, 118*a*. Charmet 75, 92, 93, 94, 95, 97, 100, 107, 114*a*, 114-15*b*, 158, 160, 180, 183, 188, 195*l*, 197. © Cosmopress Geneva ADAGP Paris *cover*. Dagli-Orti 10, 11, 13*a*, 15*l*, 22, 23, 26, 27, 32-3, 34-5, 36-7, 42, 43*a*, 51, 52*l*, 53, 60*b*, 62, 65, 66, 72, 73, 83, 96, 98-9, 101, 103, 110-11, 114, 119, 124. Rights reserved 14, 17*r*, 18*r*, 28-9*b*, 40*r*, 47*r*, 58, 60*a*, 91*r*, 120, 125, 136, 138, 139, 153*a*, 153*b*, 154, 155, 169*a*, 170, 171, 172*a*, 172*b*, 173, 174*l*, 174-175, 177*r*, 178, 179, 195*r*, 198. Ahn and Sim Rock Publications 156. Peters Publications 152. Explorer/Archives 43, 50, 85, 106*a*, 112*a*, 112*b*. Explorer/Beuzen 59*a*. Explorer/Valetin 126. Explorer/Weisbecker 68*b*. Giraudon 41, 44. Giraudon/Lauros 108, 108-9, 113. Thomas Höpker 130, 131. Josse 20, 21, 30a. Kamisuki Chokoki 174-5. Laurents 133. Roland Michaud 184. National Museum, Taipei 177*l*. Perino/Chomon 31. Reunion des Musees Nationaux 12-13b, 16, 17*l*, 18*l*, 19, 24, 25, 30b, 38, 39, 45*l*, 49. Denys Riout, Dominique Gurdjian, Jean-Pierre Leroux 130. Emil Ruder 142, 143. © SPADEM Paris 1987 140. Universal A.G. 157a, 157b. Roger Viollet 52b, 61, 81, 159, 182, 185, 187. Viollet/Alinari 40*l*. Map on pp. 70-1: James Prunier.

ACKNOWLEDGMENTS

Fayard Dessain et Tolra 184-5; Erec 174-9; Flammarion 169-73, 181-2; Gallimard 132-3, 136-8, 152-7, 162-4; Imprimerie Nationale, Paris 158-61; Arthur Niggli Verlag 139-44.

Georges Jean
was born in Besançon in 1920.
A former pupil of the
Ecole Normale Supérieure de Saint-Cloud,
he was professor of linguistics and semiology
at the University of Maine
from 1967 to 1981.
He has published some forty works,
including eight collections of poems,
essays on poetic and teaching theory
and several poetry anthologies.
He was awarded the
1980 Fondation de France prize
for *Le Plaisir des Mots,*
and in 1985 received the
Louise-Labé prize
for *D'Entre les mots.*

© Gallimard 1987

English translation © Thames and Hudson Ltd,
London, and Harry N. Abrams, Inc., New York,
1992

Reprinted 1992, 1994

Translated by Jenny Oates

Printed and bound in Italy by
Editoriale Libraria, Trieste